THE HOME FRONT

PATRICK NUTTGENS
THE HOME FRONT

HOUSING THE PEOPLE 1840-1990

BBC BOOKS

Also by Patrick Nuttgens

Reginald Fairlie, Scottish Architect
Living in Towns
York: City Buildings
Landscape of Ideas
York: the Continuing City
Leeds Old and New
Pocket Guide to World Architecture
World's Great Architecture (editor)
The Story of Architecture
Mackintosh and His Contemporaries (general editor)
What Should We Teach and How Should We Teach It?
Understanding Modern Architecture

Chapters in

Towards a Church Architecture
Higher Education: Patterns of Change in the 1970s
Spirit of the Age
Shell Guide to English Villages (Yorkshire)

Published by BBC Books
a division of BBC Enterprises Limited,
Woodlands, 80 Wood Lane, London W12 0TT

First published 1989
© Patrick Nuttgens 1989
ISBN 0 563 20714 0

Set in 11 on 13pt Century Light by Phoenix Photosetting, Chatham
Printed and bound in Great Britain by
Mackays of Chatham PLC, Chatham, Kent
Jacket printed by Belmont Press, Northampton

CONTENTS

The Home Front is based on a series of six 40 minute documentaries made by BBC North East, Leeds for BBC 2.

I am indebted to Florence Minnis for her research work on *The Home Front*, and to Evelyn Foster who helped me write the first draft of the book.

Thanks are also owed to the great number of people who have been consulted during the course of the project especially the friends and colleagues with whom I have discussed it either personally or by telephone. These include: Professor David Donnison, Sir Robert Grieve, Sir Andrew Derbyshire, Donal Crawley, Wyndham Thomas, Oliver Cox, Kenneth Campbell, Sir Donald Barron, Richard Best and John Poulson, who gave me a tour of housing in and near Pontefract and shared with me his incomparable knowledge of housing types, finance and management. My thanks also to the many City Architects and Housing Managers approached, who were unfailingly helpful and co-operative.

Edmund Cooney and Patricia Tindale read through the book in its penultimate form and made comments and amendments, many of which have been incorporated. However, the final version has been wholly written by me and I am responsible for any errors, omissions and all judgements.

Patrick Nuttgens

CHAPTER ONE

HOUSING: A PLACE TO LIVE

Just using a house is part of everybody's personal history. The chances are that it is in a house that we are born and make love and (preferably) die. We may use a house to work and certainly play; in houses of different sorts we may learn and teach and worship; we may think and talk and make things and care for people.

In finding a house, moving into one and leaving it, buying or selling or renting it, we each have a story to tell—and, with only a little encouragement, will insist on telling it. It is in a house that we (with any luck) wake up in the morning, go in and out during the day and return to sleep (with any luck) at night.

Of all the buildings that we make and use, it is difficult to think of any that matters more to us—and matters in a profoundly personal way. There is no kind of building that we know more about—and yet know less about. The fact is that we take it too much for granted.

There always has been—and probably always will be—a housing crisis. When George Orwell asked a miner when the housing shortage first became acute in his district, the miner replied, 'When we were told about it.' The difference between today and any previous period in history is that we know much more about it.

There are, for example, about 5000 million people in the world today and of them, according to a recent study by the Vatican, more than 1000 million—that is, a fifth of the human race—do not have a decent place to live in. More than 100 million do not have a roof over their heads.

There must be something like 1000 million houses in the world. This country has about 22 million of them. It is, of course, one of the most prosperous and comfortable countries in the world, incomparably better housed than hundreds of others. Even so, there are still more than 100 000 families without a home and over a million houses that are said to be unfit for human habitation.

This book, and the programmes which accompany it, are not about great houses—the castles and palaces which are well known and, in varying degrees, well looked after. It is about what came to be known in the nineteenth century as *housing* rather than *houses*. This was a word that found its way first into parliamentary reports and then into Acts of Parliament—the Housing of the Working Classes Acts of 1890, 1900 and 1919. The phrase 'working classes' was significant; it was not dropped from the Acts until 1949. It indicated—and the Acts might not have been passed by Parliament if the concept had not been built in—that the houses referred to in the Acts were for the poor and under-privileged.

For 'housing' as opposed to simply 'houses' indicates a process concerned with more than the construction of houses: a process in which the financing, planning, construction and administration of dwellings is thought of as a whole. That indicates an important area of responsibility. It implies that there existed—and still exists—a need which is more than just shelter. Throughout history people have usually found shelter for themselves—houses of one kind or another, in all kinds of circumstances. Current thinking has at least two main themes. We have a need or a demand which either cannot or is unlikely to be satisfied by the ordinary operation of the market. And (possibly one of the most lasting achievements of our time) we recognise that we have a moral responsibility to the people in need. Housing has come to be seen as a *social service*. Housing, in other words, is not just about houses; housing is about *people*.

But there are a number of different ways in which that service can be rendered, and they have changed significantly during the last hundred years and may be in the midst of changing now even more dramatically. The young couple getting married today—if indeed they decide to get married rather than just set up home together— are no longer, like their parents and ancestors, looking immediately for a house in which to set up home and sooner or later start a family. The pattern has altered. Of all households in 1987 only about one in four consisted of a married couple and dependent children. Of the new households being formed the nuclear family represents less than one in twelve. And—it may sadly be remarked—one in three of the marriages being contracted today will break up within three years. It is wonderful that we bother to get married at all, and still apparently believe in marriage as an institution.

The average household, in other words, no longer consists of a breadwinning man, a housewife and several children. The average household size has declined from 3.09 in 1962 to 2.55 in 1987. That reflects the fact that a considerable number of new households are single parent families or single people. Many unmarried sons and daughters who used to live at home now maintain separate bases. Furthermore, marriage takes place earlier and fewer married couples remain in the parental home. The increase in the number of marriages, together with an increase in the divorce rate and a reduction in family size, has led to a greater number of smaller domestic units. The standard household size has declined; the number of households has risen.

More households than ever before are elderly—four times more than in 1901. And ethnic groups have created new demands for new types of dwelling.

But first it is necessary to look briefly at the basic component for all social housing: the ordinary house. What is remarkable about it is that once it had taken shape—by about the end of the nineteenth century—it changed very little. What changed was sometimes its size, more often its grouping, density, environment and cost.

The ordinary dwelling in this country consists of one or two spaces for living, one for eating and one for cooking, several spaces for sleeping, a space for bathing and one for excreting. There may also be a number of spaces for storing and saving goods and clothes and anything worth keeping. Many of these spaces were not always necessary; the most primitive dwellings were caves or huts, single or complex, under one roof or lots of roofs; and all the facilities were not always regarded as necessary—for most of human history people have managed without toilets.

What brought those requirements together—at first as desirable, eventually as essential—was the Industrial Revolution, affecting towns and cities and then the whole of the countryside. After much experience and experiment, the pattern that came to be acceptable was a dwelling that would consist of a living room, a dining room (possibly combined), a kitchen (possibly combined with dining), a bathroom and toilet, and either one bedroom (for a single person or a couple), two or commonly three (one for the parents, one for the boys and one for the girls).

In most countries, and certainly in this country, the dwelling has to be heated. That meant originally at least one fireplace in the living room, later central heating with or without a fireplace. In recent years the biggest change in the provision of furnishings and fittings is probably the arrival of the television set, instead of, or close to, the fireplace. You once gathered round a fire; now you gather round the TV set. It is only one of many gadgets. The revolution in housekeeping started with the vacuum cleaner in the inter-war years. Now the technology includes cookers of many kinds, refrigeration, washing machines, driers and many other labour-saving devices.

Yet despite those innovations, the basic house type has changed surprisingly little. What has changed more significantly is the distribution and size of the families or groups needing accommodation.

The housing scene changed rapidly in the years following the Second World War. It was a fundamental change. At the time of the Housing Act of 1919, which for the first time created subsidies for housing, it was assumed that the type of house needed was first and foremost a family house, with one bedroom for the parents, one for the boys and one for the girls—an assumption confirmed in many studies and reports before and since. The minimum standard house was therefore a three-bedroom house. If possible it would also have two living rooms—a general one and a parlour. That quickly got reduced to one, and stayed there.

But what of the overall supply of housing? As a result of the huge growth in local authority housing after the war there are now over 6 million houses in the local authority sector. Of all houses, one third are at least 60 years old. Nearly 90 per cent of those built between 1871 and 1918 are still in use. The situation is deteriorating.

The fact is that despite one of the biggest programmes of house building ever known, and despite some of the most advanced legislation in the history of the world, we have solved our housing problem no more successfully than any other country. It may be that it is getting worse.

There are still in this country more than 100 000 homeless families, even though there are some 600 000 unoccupied dwellings. Of the others more than a million houses are officially described as being 'unfit for human habitation'. To make them fit (or at least fitter than they are) would cost, it is estimated, between £12 and £24 billion. To replace them, which is what we have been doing until recently, would cost a lot more. But we probably shan't replace them.

There has been a dramatic reversal of our attitudes towards housing and we may well prefer to keep the ones we have and try to rehabilitate them. We have—somewhat belatedly—come to recognise the value of keeping a community together. The advantages are not only social; they include factors affecting the incidence of vanda-

An aerial view of Plymouth with old houses in foreground. New roads cut swathes through the remnants of older streets that survived the bombing.

lism and crime. So more existing houses will survive—even though 1 in 14 is said to be overcrowded.

Needs have changed since the war and so have policies. In the immediate aftermath of the war it seemed that the greatest need would be caused by the destruction by bombing. Famous among the towns wrecked by bombing in the early years of the war were Coventry, Hull and Plymouth. The transformation thereafter was, however, as much the result of policies as of bombing.

The rebuilding was sometimes uninspired and sometimes imaginative. Within a few days of the bombing of Coventry, the city architect was able to present to his council plans for rebuilding the city on which his colleagues had been working for several years. And the housing was different from anything seen there before.

Other cities were less fortunate. Both Hull and Plymouth were marred by unimaginative replanning and most of the housing was similarly bleak and uninteresting. But it did result in some overdue slum clearance and reflected the aspirations for better housing of those who had travelled abroad and wanted to see improvements. They were in any case now citizens of the Welfare State.

Possibly more lasting in its effect than the bombing was the social change accompanied by political changes after the war. Throughout the war constant publicity had been given to the fact that the desirable post-war reconstructed society would be a *planned* one. And who more appropriate to carry out such a series of plans than a Labour government elected by an overwhelming majority immediately at the end of the war?

As we look at the results of 40 years of planning and reconstruction we can hardly fail to be aware of marked contrasts that have resulted from the same programmes and the same planning.

Some of the new housing erected in this country since the Second World War has been triumphantly successful; some has been a disaster; still other schemes at present under construction promise to be both provocative and fascinating.

Among the most successful of all local authority projects was that for Byker in Newcastle. In 1968 the local authority retained the Swedish architect Ralph Erskine as planner and architect for the housing. His first step was to establish a site office in a disused funeral parlour on the site. What was involved was the replacement of over 2000 dwellings in what had come to be a slum neighbourhood.

Byker, Newcastle. Social housing at its best. Effectively a village in modern (and somewhat Scandinavian) idiom, with colourful houses inside the famous Wall, designed to exclude traffic noise

Below and right Hulme, Manchester. Social housing at its worst. Stained grey concrete and barren wastes. Ironically, John Nash Crescent (below) recalls the great architect of London's Regency Terraces.

Erskine and his team consulted everyone, noted all the comments from residents, and tried—generally successfully—to recreate the community on the same site. It was a prize-winning scheme and its variety was remarkable. At one end was the tall sweep of wonderfully silhouetted housing on the skyline, the Byker Wall, shielding most of the site from the noise expected from a planned urban motorway; within the site, terraced and grouped lower houses on land thickly planted with trees and shrubs. The residents speak of it with much enthusiasm and very few criticisms.

A notable contrast is with a scheme of similar size—the Hulme estate in Manchester, an inner city development close to the educational precinct with the university and polytechnic. That consists of nearly 5000 dwellings, mostly with deck access, some in crescents named after the great architects of the eighteenth century—Kent and Hawksmoor and Nash. It is not a happy place, desperately in need of maintenance and now of renewal, embarrassingly uncared for and unpopular with almost everyone.

Of the schemes involving the renewal of existing and often
decayed areas, one of the most remarkable has been at Wirksworth in
Derbyshire. By the mid-seventies Wirksworth seemed to have no
future. The shopping and recreational facilities were poor, unemployment was high, the town looked shabby and depressing. Eight
years later, after work by both the local authority and the Civic Trust,
the town had been transformed. Derelict buildings had been refurbished, the environment generally cleaned up, shopping and recreation facilities improved, new jobs created and some excellent
housing produced, both new and restored. The work received a
Europa Nostra Award in 1982.

Of the work at present in progress the most spectacular and
varied is that of the London Docklands, one of the largest regene-
ration schemes in Europe. The deserted docks, a derelict wasteland
of corrugated iron fences and sheds and empty buildings, where
more than 20 000 jobs had disappeared in 10 years, have been transformed under the aegis of the London Docklands Development Corporation. 12 000 new houses have been built and the number is
expected to double by 1990. These are in the main expensive—
sometimes very expensive—houses and flats and in no way solve the
problem of what has come to be known as 'affordable' housing. But
the results are already fascinating and in at least one case—the
Cascades—spectacular.

Housing has, however, always been more than some spectacular
architectural ventures. To understand those projects and their social
significance, it is necessary to look at some of the underlying changes
that have occurred in the years during the present century which,
after all, gave birth to the great housing movement.

First (and ultimately crucial) is the fact that there has been a
total reversal in the tenure of houses. In 1901 90 per cent of all
houses were rented, that is, rented (with a few exceptions) from private owners. By 1946, at the end of the Second World War, and
despite a boom in building by speculative builders between the two
wars, more than 60 per cent of the population still lived in privately
rented accommodation. By 1988 only 10 per cent of houses were privately rented. Slum clearance, rent controls and tenants' rights had
reduced them.

What of the rest? About a third of the houses (say 30 per cent)
are now rented from local authorities, the result of the great age of
council building, at first between the wars, more dramatically after

the Second World War. But the biggest change has been the growth in owner-occupation. Now 60 per cent of houses are owner-occupied—that is, mainly bought by means of mortgages. If present trends continue, including the sale of council houses to their tenants which was given new impetus by the Act of 1980, the owner-occupied sector will reach 70 per cent. The aim of the present government may be to bring it up to 90 per cent, though there is reason to doubt that that will ever be achieved.

In round figures (which are easier to understand than percentages), of the 22 million houses in the United Kingdom, private houses account for about 13 million, privately rented houses for 2 million, local authority housing for 6 million. Finally, more than half a million are the work of Housing Associations. It seems that the main trends have been first away from privately rented to local authority renting, then from local authority renting to private ownership.

Why does this matter? Looking back for a moment to the setting up of local authority housing, it seems to be the case that one of the most fundamental reasons for governments to promote and (in varying policies) find money for housing was *fear*. Such fears were frequently expressed towards the end of and after the First World War, vividly by Lloyd George, who recognised that good housing was crucial to the stability of the state: new houses should be 'Homes fit for Heroes'.

That was more than just a negative precaution arising from fear and anxiety. It coincided with the awakening social conscience that may have become an ideal. Addressing representatives of local authorities in Buckingham Palace in 1919, King George V made an unusually positive statement:

> The housing problem is not a new problem. It is an old problem, which has been aggravated by the past five years of war, and which the forced neglect of those five grim years has rendered so acute as to constitute a grave national danger if it is not promptly and energetically tackled. ... There is no question at present of greater social importance than the housing of the working classes. ... It is not too much to say that an adequate solution to the housing question is the foundation of all social progress. Health and housing are indissolubly connected.

And he made a final telling point:

> If 'unrest' is to be converted into contentment the provision of good houses may prove one of the most potent agents in that conversion.

Because, as more than a few writers and speakers confirmed time and time again, in a cry that increased through the later years of the nineteenth century and reached a crescendo of anxiety and purpose after the Great War, there cannot be a more fundamental, just and (you might think) painfully obvious social obligation upon any civilised society—and certainly upon any society that lays claim to moral beliefs in social justice and social concern—than the conviction that every member of society should have access to a decent dwelling. In other words, that however free anyone should be to reject it, there should be a place available for everyone.

It is one of the more extraordinary facts about Victorian society that most of the great and prosperous industrialists should have been able to ignore what common sense and the ordinary dictates of a Christian conscience should have told them anyway: that their workers ought to be able to live in reasonable conditions—better for them, for society and, of course, for profits. And, indeed, as we shall see in the next chapter, some of the more philanthropic manufacturers did obey conscience and common sense, ensuring that they would have a healthy and contented work force.

Looking back with the hindsight of today and within the context of half a century of social progress, I still find the aspiration of the caring members of the professions and of public authorities one of the great exercises in social idealism. The determination that there should be a fit and healthy home for everyone must be one of the greatest ideals in history. It is so obvious that it sounds rather dull and undramatic; it is so obvious that it ought to be taken for granted. The evidence of history past and even present shows that it cannot be.

The next development which led to a major re-think about the responsibilities and triumphs was this: that while old houses easily become slums if they are not loved and maintained, some of today's slums are made up of new houses. It is one of the many ironies of social building that some of the mass housing erected in the last 30 years to replace the slums that were demolished to make room for them are now slums themselves. Some of the most unfit housing is the very housing erected to make sure that no housing was unfit.

So policies have been changed. Fewer flats are now being erected. More attention is being paid to maintenance. Alterations are taking place to mass schemes and the main emphases are towards the refurbishment of existing housing. Some of that must be caused by lack of capital. But it also reflects a deeper fact—that we are no longer so confident about what is fit and desirable housing. A move towards private ownership and towards tenant co-operation may be easier than deciding what ought to be a modern house. Let the new owners and tenants decide for themselves.

But at the end of it all is money. The famous Victorian slums were closely packed houses erected quickly and cheaply for the working classes in the dramatically expanding cities. They were of course no worse than the hovels in agricultural districts from which those very people were only too anxious to escape as they flocked to the towns in search of jobs and money. The inadequacies of rural housing weren't so obvious because it was remote and because people died younger; their houses just dissolved into the landscape. The vastly growing industrial cities demanded attention. Hence the Public Health Acts which were provoked by the cities but never by agricultural conditions, however dreadful.

There never has been equality in the world and I doubt if there ever will be: individuality and energy will ensure inequality whatever the conditions. But there must surely be a quantifiable minimum standard of living below which we cannot go. And it must rise as people's expectations rise.

Yet it seems that no one has yet discovered a way to bring houses—*housing*—within the reach of the ordinary working man or woman without public subsidy—without the state in one form or another finding money to pay for conditions that will make possible a reasonable life. And there is no evidence that it will be possible now.

We must therefore ask whether it is possible to define that problem more clearly. I believe there was a relatively recent period in this country when the problem of good housing was successfully tackled—written about, tried and recorded. To that attempt we must now turn.

CHAPTER TWO

THE PURSUIT
OF ENVIRONMENT

If, as King George V declared: 'It is not too much to say that an adequate solution to the housing question is the foundation of all social progress', it is clearly necessary to ask what was the nature of the 'housing question' as the King and his advisers saw it in 1919. They could not have seen it as just one of the many casualties of the war; they must have recognised that its roots went deeper into history. It was in fact one of the many legacies of the drastic, and sometimes tempestuous changes of the previous century.

These changes concerned not only the fabric of the houses, but the total context in which they existed. Any solution must therefore involve the total environment of living and working. It must require at least an idea. The attempts to find a total solution in the latter part of the nineteenth century and the early years of the twentieth century I have therefore called 'the pursuit of environment'.

For whatever the hard facts and the numerical problems of the housing needs and housing policies, it is impossible to understand the history of housing and its social meaning without recognising the idealism that inspired the movement for reform. Idealism is a difficult concept to play with in the present day, and it may be that the majority of people have never experienced it and wouldn't recognise it if it was in front of their noses. But there can be little doubt that it was a profound idealism that shaped the housing of the best period of innovation and concern.

What profoundly affected both the problem and the concern about it was the Industrial Revolution, born in this country in the hundred years from 1750 to 1850, and effectively transforming first this country and then the whole of the world. By the last half of the nineteenth century the congestion and blight of the great cities into which people had poured in the preceding hundred years was an obvious scandal. The houses might be no worse—and might indeed be better—than the agricultural cottages or hovels from which people had hurried in search of work to the industrial cities. But the cities presented problems of housing more acute than any village.

Some of the worst were, as Mrs Gaskell described them in *North and South*, the industrial towns of the north.

> For several miles before they reached Milton, they saw a deep lead-coloured cloud hanging over the horizon. ... Quick they were whirled over long, straight, hopeless streets of regularly built houses. ... Here and there a great oblong many-windowed factory stood up ... puffing out black 'unparliamentary' smoke.

A similar industrial town was created by Dickens in *Hard Times*:

> Coketown was 'a town of red brick', or a brick that would have been red if the smoke and ashes had allowed it. It was a town of machinery and tall chimneys. ... It had a black canal in it, and a river that ran purple with ill-smelling dye. ... Nature was as strongly bricked out as killing airs and gases were bricked in.

The housing problem was notably acute in the towns that had experienced the initial impact of industrialisation. Manchester and Liverpool and the surrounding cotton towns were especially badly affected. The condition of Manchester was lamented by both reformers and novelists. Dr James Phillips Kay gave an account of the accommodation of the Manchester cotton workers in 1832: 'The houses in such situations are uncleanly, ill-provided with furniture. ... they are often dilapidated, hardly drained, damp.'

It was not surprising. Manchester increased in population by 47 per cent between 1821 and 1831; Bradford increased by 78 per cent in the same period. Engels gave a colourful description of one of the worst areas in Salford in 1844:

> The working-men's dwellings between Oldfield Road and Cross Lane ... are in the worst possible state ... [they] vie with the dwellings of the Old Town in filth and overcrowding. In this district I found a man, apparently sixty years old, living in a cow-stable.

While money was spent to embellish town centres with civic buildings, or cleanse streets in prosperous areas, little or nothing was done to improve the poorer districts. Dr Southwood Smith, reporting to the Poor Law Commissioners in 1839, talked of 'the filthy, close and crowded conditions' that the poor lived in, and of 'the dreadful evils to which they are exposed'.

The smell, with overflowing sewage and bodies close together, must have been almost unbearable, even in a less hygiene-conscious age. One Irish tenant said that the court he inhabited in Leeds was 'inundated with filth, having a most intolerable stench proceeding from two ash-pits in the adjoining courts having oozed through the wall.' The smell, he said, was enough to raise the roof off his skull.

In the old port of Hull, in the dock area, where interconnecting courts had only one entrance to the road, six weeks' accumulation of 'night-soil' was dragged through houses where people were at breakfast.

But it was generally agreed that Glasgow had some of the worst conditions. Edwin Chadwick, the reformer, reported of his visit:

> There were no privies or drains ... and the dungheaps received all filth which the swarm of wretched inhabitants could give; and we learnt that a considerable part of the rent of the houses was paid by the produce of the dungheaps.

In Dundee in 1847, a woman taking a flat was shown a locked wall cupboard and told she could use it if she wished to clean it out. It turned out to be crammed with dung. She declined the offer.

Both physically and socially, cellar dwellings were considered to be the lowest form of accommodation. They were almost always described as dark, damp, filthy and airless. Mrs Gaskell gives a vivid account of a Manchester cellar in her first novel, *Mary Barton*:

> You went down one step even from the foul area into the cellar.... It was very dark inside. The window panes were broken and stuffed with rags. . .. the smell was so foetid as to knock the two men down.... they began to penetrate the thick darkness of the place, and to see three or four little children rolling on the damp, nay wet, brick floor, through which the moisture of the street oozed up.

Peter Gaskell, in his *Manufacturing Population of England* (1833), also writing about Manchester, corroborated the novelist's account: 'These cellars are the very picture of loathsomeness.... they speedily become disgusting receptacles of every species of vermin that can affect the human body.'

Back-to-back houses were theoretically superior to cellars, in that they were specifically designed for the working class. They were the speculative builders' answer to mass demand. The classic description of the back-to-back was supplied by Edwin Chadwick in the famous *Report on the Sanitary Condition of the Labouring Population* (1842):

> The walls are only half brick thick, or what the bricklayers call a brick noggin, and the whole of the materials are slight and unfit for the purpose.... they are built back to back; without ventilation or drainage; and like a honeycomb, every particle of space is occupied.

The houses, as their name implies, backed on to one another in a confined space, thus making the spread of disease more likely. The Committee of the Board of Health set up to research housing defects in Nottingham was disbanded in 1833 only a year after its formation, when the cholera threat had disappeared; but in that time it had made some useful discoveries. It found 8000 back-to-back houses with no through ventilation and only one convenience for several dwellings. Many of the streets outside were neither paved nor drained.

Contrary to popular belief, and despite the purer quality of the air, housing in the country was as troubled as that in the cities. In rural areas the number of people had increased, as indeed it had in the towns; at the same time the number of cottages had dwindled. This led to chronic overcrowding in much the same manner as in the cities. In 1843 the *Report on the Employment of Women and Children in Agriculture* gave gruesome accounts of 29 people under one roof, of 11 adults in one small bedroom, of holes in roofs and women having babies on floors.

The Victorians were characteristically concerned about what effects this overcrowding would have on morals. The Honourable and Reverend Sidney Godolphin Osborne, rector of Bryanston near Blandford, expressed his strongest disapproval, even if he balked at the details:

> I do not choose to put on paper the disgusting scenes that I have known to occur from this promiscuous crowding of the sexes together. Seeing, however, to what the mind of the young female is exposed to from her very childhood, I have long ceased to wonder at the otherwise seeming precocious licentiousness of conversation which may be heard in every field where many of the young are at work together.

There were two further dimensions to the problem. First, the age of the housing stock worried the Victorians as it does us, if to a lesser extent, today. Cottages that had been inadequate in the seventeenth and eighteenth centuries were still being used in the nineteenth. Some of them were, in William Cobbett's words, 'little better than pig-beds'.

The second factor, also familiar today, was that the rents were generally more than the (poorer) working man could afford. A witness before the 1824 Committee on Labourers complained: 'The rent of the cottages is so high that it is one of the chief causes of the agricultural labourers being in a worse state than they ever were.'

The Victorians made the mistake—and it is possible to make the same mistake again today—of believing that it was irrelevant to concern themselves with the housing of the poorest. They argued that by concentrating on the homes of the better off, those at the bottom would eventually benefit by a cumulative improvement of standards.

What then was to be done? The protest about housing came not from the sufferers themselves but from the relatively privileged—the politicians, writers, reformers and idealists. It became increasingly clear, as the nineteenth century progressed, that the matter was urgent. Medical officers realised that demolition without rehousing only displaced the problem elsewhere. It was of no help simply to demolish insanitary buildings if there was no alternative available. The Health Officer for Hackney claimed that by implementing the overcrowding clauses of the 1866 Sanitary Act, he was sentencing 10 000 people to sleep in the streets. Legislation against overcrowding was useful, but unless more houses were built its enforcement would cause widespread homelessness.

That had also been one of the causes of the housing crisis in the countryside. Unfit cottages had been knocked down, but new ones had not been built in their place: this created a shortage. In the city, houses had been destroyed to make way for street improvements, new offices and railway lines, again without reconstruction.

But overall, by the late 1870s, overcrowding and the housing problem were being viewed as ultimately questions of poverty. What was needed above all was money, and it was the lack of money which forced people, as it still does, to live in slums or to go without a home altogether.

In 1874, the Royal College of Physicians presented a petition to the Prime Minister. It identified poverty and high rents as the chief culprits of the housing crisis, and condemned the work of philanthropists as woefully inadequate. But in fact the philanthropists were the pioneers of improved housing, and their work preceded legislation and the work of the public authority.

The first celebrated vision was that of James Silk Buckingham, who in 1849 published his proposals for an ideal city named 'Victoria'. It was to have 25 000 inhabitants, be built on 1000 acres of ground and be surrounded by an agricultural estate. It was intended to achieve 'order, symmetry, space and healthfulness', and to effect 'the comfort and convenience of all classes'. One way to achieve this was to avoid overcrowding by insisting on low densities—the number of

New Lanark, built between 1784 and 1796 by Dale and Owen, who were trying to find a new and healthy environment for industrial workers. The upper reaches of the Clyde supplied power for the mills.

people per acre. Although 'Victoria' was never built, many of its ideas were realised by later reformers.

Some of the earliest practical experiments were made in the north of England and in Scotland. New Lanark, a cotton spinning manufactory, was founded on a site near the Falls of Clyde in 1784 by David Dale, a Glasgow banker and industrialist. Richard Arkwright, the inventor of the waterframe, was involved with the venture.

To work his mill Dale needed labourers, and to obtain them he had to build a town. He took 500 children from the Edinburgh Workhouse and built a large new house for them. In order to attract adults as well, he built a number of low rent houses. By 1796 he had

four mills in operation employing 1340 hands, 750 of them children. Half of these were under nine years old. Dale was a kind master and living conditions were generally regarded as excellent, if only in comparison with conditions generally at the time. But New Lanark is mainly associated with the work of Robert Owen.

Owen met the Dales in 1792. Within the year, Owen had purchased the mill, married Dale's daughter Rose and taken over New Lanark. He was committed to the good of the people as well as that of the business. During his time at New Lanark he initiated important reforms. He built a grocery shop, vegetable market, school, bakery and wash house for his employees.

He also set up an Institute for the Formation of Character. Every morning calisthenics were held there. The preachers termed it 'immoral dancing'. He improved the existing houses and built new ones to higher standards. They had large rooms, good windows and solid walls. He went further. Owen desired not only to better his workers' environment, but also to mend their characters. He read them lectures on ethics and imposed fines for drunkenness and hangovers.

More constructively Owen took the children between five and ten years old from the mill and put them to school full-time. He was convinced that social conditions affected character, but also that it was possible to be humane and still excel in business terms. Indeed he made a handsome profit. More than that, he showed that success was not dependent on crowding large numbers of people together in vast towns.

Overcrowding was at its most dense in the wool and worsted manufacturing centres of the West Riding of Yorkshire—the prodigy towns of the Industrial Revolution. The men who set out to improve them were manufacturers who hoped to create an environment in keeping with social ideals. Their motives were, of course, mixed. They involved both self-interest and benevolence: the health and well-being of the residents would encourage more efficient organisation, which would in turn ensure regularity of work.

Colonel Edward Akroyd, MP for Halifax, was one of the early improvers. His first model village was Copley, built between 1844 and 1853, two miles south of Halifax. The houses were back-to-back, the church was neo-Gothic.

Akroyd's essay *On Improved Dwellings for the Working Classes* contains a description of Copley:

> A picturesque outline was adopted in a modified Old English style, approximating to the character of many old dwellings in the neighbourhood, and also in harmony with the beautiful site. ... In front of the cottages, facing the river are allotment gardens, flanked by a recreation ground; and on the bank is seated the village school with its separate play yards. In the opposite site it is proposed to erect a church. ... A classroom serves for the village library and newsroom.

The major disadvantage was that Copley houses were the infamous back-to-back type. Many had only one living room downstairs and only one bedroom upstairs. Akroyd defended himself by saying that back-to-backs were the common style and that many people only

Brambles, wild roses, children and dogs enjoy Akroydon's Victorian cemetery, a common land for past and present residents.

wanted one bedroom anyway. The *Builder*, in its review of Copley, was less tolerant: 'There can be no apology for back-to-back houses, and though it is one of the common features of the country ... we believe strong efforts are now being made to put a stop to the practice.' It conceded that the Copley houses were the best of the type to be found in Yorkshire, and admitted furthermore that such housing, whilst always undesirable, was less damaging in the country than in the town.

Akroyd's second and more ambitious experiment was at Akroydon, started in 1861 near the centre of Halifax. In Akroydon the social purpose of the early model villages was more apparent. The houses, which were at different price levels, were deliberately arranged to promote the mixing of social classes. The houses were generally two-storey, positioned round a green, and built of stone with slate roofs. They had a large living room, a scullery or wash kitchen, a main bedroom and children's bedroom. Later houses were more spacious with a parlour and a third bedroom.

Akroydon's architect was the celebrated George Gilbert Scott. Akroyd related:

> In 1859 I consulted the eminent architect Mr George Gilbert Scott and commissioned him to furnish plans and designs in the domestic Gothic. This type was adopted not solely for the gratification of my own taste, but because it is the original of the parish of Halifax, over which many old houses are scattered of the date of the Commonwealth, or shortly after.

The idea was not only to build sanitary dwellings but to alert the people's minds to beauty. The Gothic form was considered the most appropriate medium for this. Perhaps most importantly of all, at Akroydon he introduced a scheme of home ownership. The first Building Society, the Halifax Union, had been founded in 1845—popularly known as the 'Go-a-head Society'. Akroyd's Building Association, capitalised by the Halifax Union, was set up in 1860.

The Association supplied three-quarters of the house cost; the future owner had to find a quarter. It was an arrangement which was beneficial to all. Under the Parliamentary Reform Act of 1832, and the Municipal Corporations Act of 1835, a householder needed a 40 shilling freehold in order to have a vote. The Building Society arranged the freehold; Akroyd expected the vote.

The most celebrated work of the philanthropic improvers was Saltaire, north of Bradford, built between 1850 and 1863—the creation of the Bradford alpaca manufacturer, Sir Titus Salt.

Saltaire was on a massive baronial scale in Italian Renaissance style. In moving his works from Bradford, Sir Titus wanted not just housing, but a town that would be self-sufficient. He built his factory, whose length equalled that of St Paul's Cathedral, first, and the cottages ten years later.

The village also included 45 almshouses, an institute, a school, a church and a 14 acre park on the other side of the River Aire. The cottages were models of their kind. They had a living room, scullery and two to four bedrooms. Water and gas were supplied, and each had a private yard with privy, coal store and ashpit. None of the houses were back-to-back.

Salt had carried out a detailed survey of his employees' housing needs. He instructed his architects, Lockwood and Mason of Bradford, that 'nothing should be spared to render the dwellings of the operatives a pattern to the country.' At his own expense he provided amenities that included chapels, reading rooms, public baths and a gymnasium with a Turkish bath.

Left Sir Titus Salt's great mill beside the river, the canal and the railway of Saltaire. Sir Titus supplied houses, almshouses, a school and a hospital. *Below* Port Sunlight.

Salt was particularly averse to clutter, and wanted to avoid the untidiness caused by washing hanging across the street to dry. In 1839 the Leeds Corporation Statistical Report had said that in Leeds half the streets were 'so full of lines and linen as to be impassable for horses and carriages and almost for foot passengers.'

To avoid such untidiness in his settlement, Sir Titus set up a steam laundry which operated at very low prices. Clothes, he stipulated, were to be dried in back yards and not hung across the street. Sir Titus himself rode around the town on horseback carrying a swordstick. If he saw any washing hanging in the street to dry he would slash the clothesline and bring the washing down to the ground.

Salt's example was followed by other wealthy industrialists. Lord Lever founded Port Sunlight near Liverpool in 1888. He put into practice his vision of profit sharing; he chose to convert the workers' share of profits into improved housing rather than an annual payment. He also wanted to avoid urban uniformity: his model community contained a diversity of styles.

Port Sunlight's handsome public open spaces, better than any previous industrial village, with thoroughly English houses, friendly, humane and utterly respectable.

The houses at Port Sunlight were either semi-detached or built in groups of four to six, separated by wide, open spaces. There were low densities and large space allowances as well as a range of facilities all financed by the Lever Brothers. The Levers insisted that their village arose not from benevolence but self-interest. The annual outlay, they said, was more than compensated by high productivity and good industrial relations.

In 1879, George Cadbury decided to move his works outside Birmingham; he wanted room for expansion and cleaner conditions for food production. He went further. He built beside the factory 24 double tunnel-back houses, typical of Birmingham houses of the time. They reflected George Cadbury's philosophy that 'the best way to improve a man's circumstances is to raise his ideals. . . . How can a man cultivate ideals when his home is a slum and his only place of recreation the public house?' Like Owen, Cadbury believed that housing and mental and physical health were linked.

In 1895, that little settlement was expanded into the model vil-

lage of Bournville. In founding that, Cadbury put into action his ideal of 'alleviating the evils that arise from the insanitary and insufficient accommodation supplied to large numbers of the working classes, and of securing to the workers in factories some of the advantages of outdoor village life.'

By 1912, nearly 1000 houses had been built at Bournville. The construction followed the natural contours of the land, unlike Port Sunlight which was artificially landscaped. In doing this he introduced an important new planning principle—that houses should not cover more than a quarter of the plot. But above all, both Port Sunlight and Bournville were intended to promote good behaviour; instead of dirt and drink, they offered soap and cocoa.

Many attempts to tackle the housing problem in the nineteenth century took the form of charitable trusts. They were helped by the Labouring Classes Dwelling Houses Act of 1886, which allowed companies to borrow at reduced rates from the Public Works Loans Commissioners. The combination of loans and the general belief that they

The American philanthropist George Peabody was so shaken by the sight of London's slums that he financed blocks of housing for workers. His example was followed by others, e.g. the Sutton Trust, which built these blocks, still much in demand.

should not expect more than five per cent return on their investment formed the basis of the financial work of what came to be known as the five per cent philanthropists.

The projects were many and various and they varied in popularity. Possibly the most unsuccessful was the Total Abstainers Industrial Farm, promoted in 1883 by the Society for Promoting Industrial Villages. It attracted few enthusiasts and was quickly wound up.

In London, the Peabody Trust started in 1862 with the gift of £150 000 from an American merchant, George Peabody. It followed a different design policy. It concentrated on multi-storey blocks containing one, two and three-roomed apartments, usually with shared sinks and WCs. By 1887 the Trust had provided 5014 dwellings.

At the same time the Improved Industrial Dwellings Company was founded by Sydney Waterlow, a Londoner who had transformed his father's stationery business into a great printing house. Waterlow was interested in politics and social problems, and believed that the housing crisis was capable of solution. The IIDC built Langbourne Buildings in Finsbury in 1863. The plan was to create a housing unit for letting to artisans while making the usual five per cent profit for its owner—the basic component in a self-contained tenement with its own scullery and WC.

Waterlow said of both his financial and structural principles:

> All I have endeavoured to show is that capital expended in the erection of light, cheerful, healthy habitations for the industrial classes in crowded cities, may be made to yield a fair interest on its investment if care is taken to avoid extravagance in external architectural decoration or loss by large management expenses.

Waterlow's company, like the Peabody Trust, was criticised for failing to provide for the poorest. On the other hand, like the Trust, it explained that this was not its intention. It adhered to the philosophy of helping the poorest by aiding the wealthiest:

> It would not have been right to build down to the lowest class because you must have built a class of tenement which I hope none of them would have been satisfied with at the end of fifty years. We have tried rather to build for the best class, and by lifting them up to leave more room for the second and third who are below them.

In 1867, the Artisans, Labourers and General Dwellings Company was formed to develop suburban cottage estates. It was founded by the builder William Austin. It began as a glorified building society, but became much more. In the 1870s and 1880s the company constructed three low-rise estates, at Lavender Hill, Noel Park, Hornsey and Streatham Hill. The houses were well built and spacious. Planting trees in the streets greatly humanised the estates. Rents of seven to thirteen shillings a week secured returns of six to seven per cent, but predictably restricted accommodation to the better paid.

In contrast, the 1884 East End Dwellings Company aimed its accommodation at the poorest. It provided minimal accommodation for unskilled labourers in single units. It explained:

> The main endeavour of the company will be to provide for the poorest class of self-supporting labourers dwelling accommodation at the very cheapest rates compatible with realising a fair rate of interest upon the capital employed. Hitherto little or nothing of this kind has been done on a large scale, the buildings of the existing companies and associations being chiefly occupied by a class of industrial tenants more prosperous than those for whom this Company proposes to provide.

The East End Dwellings Company thus set out to cater for a class that all the earlier companies had ignored. The philanthropic bodies had made an admirable effort, but had only touched the surface of a massive and ever growing crisis. What their work had made clear, however, was that some kind of state aid was essential. As the London Trades Council put it to the Royal Commission formed to investigate the housing of the working classes in 1884:

> It is totally impossible that private enterprise, philanthropy and charity can ever keep pace with the present demands. . . . Economic forces and population have outstepped their endeavours; hence evils accrue. But what the individual cannot do the state municipality must seek to accomplish . . . for it alone possesses the necessary power and wealth.

What, however, fundamentally shaped the design of housing at the turn of the century was the Garden City Movement. Its pioneer was Ebenezer Howard. In 1898, he published his seminal book, *Tomorrow: A Peaceful Path to Real Reform*, re-issued a few years later as *Garden Cities of Tomorrow.*

Howard had a vision of 'slumless, smokeless cities', and introduced the idea of the 'garden city', combining the strengths of both town and country with the disadvantages of neither. It was also to be an exercise in co-operative ownership. What, in Howard's view, was needed was a magnet to lure people back to the countryside.

The Garden Cities and Town Planning Association's definition of a garden city was: 'A town planned for industry and healthy living;

of a size that makes possible the full measure of social life, but not larger; surrounded by a belt of rural land; the whole of the land being in public ownership, or held in trust for the community.'

Carefully avoiding the Utopian approach of some of the earlier reformers, Howard aimed to bring people back to the land on a sound economic basis. He suggested that garden city development companies should be formed to purchase sites and lease plots to those wishing to build. The increasing value of the land would then pass to the company, which would finance community services and municipally owned buildings. The community ownership principle was intended to avoid the paternalistic and mercenary attitudes unpopular elsewhere.

Howard looked afresh at the problem which had been troubling England since the Industrial Revolution—that of the growth and overcrowding of the cities and their fatal attraction for country people. He illustrated his idea of the existing situation and his proposals for its solution, by the diagram he described as the Three Magnets. This showed the relative merits and demerits of town and country and how the strengths of each should be joined:

> Neither the town magnet nor the country magnet represents the full plan and purpose of nature. Human society and the beauty of nature are meant to be enjoyed together. The two magnets must be made one. ... Town and country must be married, and out of this joyous union will spring a new hope, a new life, a new civilisation.

The obvious way to merge the town and country, to relieve the overcrowding pressure on the city and the unemployment pressure in rural areas, was to have a 'garden city'—a town with all the advantages of numbers and employment in the healthier and less densely populated countryside. At two garden city conferences, held at Bournville in 1901 and Port Sunlight in 1902, Howard publicly aired his scheme. It bore instant fruit in the following year (1903) when Howard's first garden city, Letchworth, was begun.

Built on virgin farmland, Letchworth was comprehensively planned to accommodate 35 000 inhabitants with four neighbourhood units, each containing public buildings, shops, schools and a recreational green. Housing density was at most 12 houses to the acre, the cottages carefully set out in short terraces and cul-de-sacs. It was a careful attempt to create a community in line with the English ideal of home. It had an organised layout of streets, alike enough to avoid disunity, different enough for individuality.

Howard's second garden city was Welwyn in Hertfordshire, built from 1919 to 1920. Its layout and housing were more ordered than Letchworth's. This greater architectural control, however, was sometimes criticised as being too 'stiff'; the houses were designed in a neo-Georgian style by the architect Louis De Soissons.

The architect responsible for Letchworth, who worked out the physical form of Howard's first ideals, was Raymond Unwin. As a boy he had heard Ruskin lecture and had met William Morris, whom he admired both as a craftsman and a socialist.

He saw, as an ideal, 'a more ordered form of society and a better planned environment for it', and had no doubt that practical planning on a human scale could only be generated by the satisfaction of the needs of people. Writing about town planning in 1909 he noted that 'miles and miles of ground which people, not yet elderly, can remember as open green fields, are now covered with dense masses of buildings packed together in rows along streets which have been laid out in a perfectly haphazard manner without any consideration for the common interest of the people'.

To understand his influence on housing, it is necessary to list the principles on which he based his ideas for garden cities and other layouts. He saw the traditional English village as a living symbol of the 'natural life' to which everyone has a right: it provided a measure of community planning. He insisted on the need to understand the past before anyone could make any appropriate plans for the future; his especial love was for the Middle Ages. He was convinced that beauty was essential for mental health:

> We have forgotten that endless rows of brick boxes looking out upon dreary streets and squalid back yards, are not really homes for people and can never become such, however complete may be the drainage system, however pure the water supply. ... Important as all these provisions are for man's material needs and sanitary existence, they do not suffice. ... There is needed the vivifying touch of art.

The consciousness of tradition was thus an integral part of the creative process. But not without criticism:

> Though the study of old towns and their buildings is most useful, nay, is almost essential to any due appreciation of the subject, we must not forget that we cannot, even if we would, reproduce the conditions under which they were created. ... While therefore we study and admire it does not follow that we can copy; for we must consider what is likely to lead to the best results under modern conditions.

But above all, Unwin was convinced that beauty was essential to mental health. By beauty he meant not ornament, but quality and harmony of form. The architect and town planner should, he said, infuse 'the spirit of the artist' into his work because 'the artist is not content with the least that will do; his desire is for the best, the utmost he can achieve. It is the small margin which makes all the difference between a thing scamped and a thing well done. . . . from this margin of welldoing beauty must spring.' He added: 'We have become so used to living among surroundings in which beauty has little or no place, that we do not realise what a remarkable and unique feature the ugliness of modern life is.' Unwin held that one of planning's chief functions was to satisfy 'the natural aesthetic hunger of mankind'.

The practical innovation specified by Unwin, confirmed in his small book *Nothing Gained by Overcrowding* and adopted by authorities after the Great War, was the rule that there should be not more than 12 houses per acre. Even in financial terms there was nothing to be gained by cramming more onto the land: the extra costs of roads outweighed any savings in land costs. High density planning was only defensible where the land was excessively costly.

The first commission undertaken by Unwin and his architect partner Barry Parker was the garden village of New Earswick, three miles north of York, started in 1901. It was started by Joseph Rowntree, though most of the development work was carried out under his son, Seebohm Rowntree.

In York there was already a surplus of housing, so the intention was not, as at Bournville, to supply desperately needed houses to those that lacked them; it was rather, as Seebohm Rowntree said, to see if housing in a congenial setting at a moderate rent was a possibility: 'It remains to be seen, therefore,' he wrote, 'whether we can build to let at a price that people will pay.' Later developments were to show the wisdom of these reservations. There were few families willing, at first, to move out of York. Transport was poor and the village grew very slowly.

But New Earswick introduced features nowadays so familiar that they are taken for granted. They include the cul-de-sac with two-storey houses grouped around it, the elimination of useless pieces of back land, reduction in the widths of road, places for children to play, houses with 'through' living rooms—so that they could be orientated in different ways without losing sunlight—the bathrooms

New Earswick was built a few miles from Rowntree's Cocoa Works. It introduced cul-de-sacs and houses grouped to promote maximum community contact.

Left and below New Earswick. Friendly brick houses, planned with great care for family life, with grass and trees, footpaths and streets named after fruit-trees.

on the first floor, the elimination of winders on the stairs, the outside store for prams and tools. It was a beautifully planned family house, and it influenced the design of housing for years to come.

The character of the early houses was simple, Unwin used traditional brick and tile construction. He achieved architectural effect by varied roof lines, prominent gables and ornamental barge-boards. He was thus able to build cheaply without monotony.

As at Bournville and Port Sunlight, houses in New Earswick were aesthetically grouped rather than regimented. Unwin evolved an organic plan which meant that the housing grew naturally out of the needs of the site. He created wider fronted houses and living rooms at the front to make the fullest use of sun and light. The whole was marked by reverence for tradition.

Raymond Unwin is a key figure in the story of housing. Artist and planner, he was a social reformer who worked with philanthropists. His influence is still apparent and even increasing. It shows in picturesque housing layouts, in good landscaping and gardens, in traditional forms of houses, in the informality and common sense which characterise contemporary English design at its best. He was in the end concerned with designing a total environment. His influence was thus far wider than his own work. It shows in the housing erected by local authorities, shaping the towns and villages of the whole country. And in particular it shows in the architecture of the post-war New Towns, which contain some of the best housing in the country and can be seen as the final legacy of the idealists.

They were based upon an idea—of a 'balanced community enjoying a full social, industrial and commercial life'—and were essentially attempts at community planning. The Commission on the New Towns was chaired by Lord Reith and reported in 1946; in that year the New Towns Act was also passed. The towns were to have a population of between 50 000 and 100 000, were to be low in density, surrounded by a green belt and thus separated from the big existing cities. In the following 40 years, altogether 25 New Towns were built, with more than 230 000 houses between them.

Most of the housing was two-storey terraced housing, in estates separated by green spaces. But the most important principle in the first generation towns was the 'neighbourhood principle'—an attempt to break down the overall size of the town into units of the right size for a community. Ten thousand people would provide enough children for a secondary modern school, two two-stream primary schools and six nursery schools; five neighbourhoods of 10 000 each would provide the right number of children for a grammar school. The school system thus became one of the determinants of social planning. The plan itself could be based upon distances appropriate for a school. At its centre the neighbourhood would have a centre with shops, a community centre and a public house. Ultimately the overall size of a neighbourhood would be dictated by the maximum walking distance for a woman with a pram.

Nearly all of these principles and devices have been rejected in subsequent years. The school system has been transformed and children travel considerable distances by bus; the family with small children is no longer the basic unit for social planning; the neighbourhood principle, if it ever indeed was realised, now sounds artificial. But the overall achievement of the New Towns remains untarnished. They produced some of the best social housing ever seen in this country—by recognising that such an aspiration must require fundamental consideration of the total community.

CHAPTER THREE

THE BIRTH OF THE COUNCIL HOUSE

On 22 February 1884 the Marquis of Salisbury moved in Parliament that a commission be set up to investigate the housing of the working classes. His proposal was an obvious response to the abuses that were becoming public and the failure of earlier legislation.

The Royal Commission on Housing was duly appointed. Its president was Sir Charles Dilke. Its members included the Prince of Wales, Cardinal Manning, Sir Richard Cross, Lord Salisbury and George Godwin. It collected vast amounts of evidence, much of it from the London Trades Council and from surveyors of a selected number of towns. The Commission reported:

> At the very outset of their inquiry Your Majesty's Commissioners had testimony to prove two important facts: first, that though there was a great improvement, described by Lord Shaftesbury as 'enormous', in the condition of the houses of the poor compared to that of 30 years ago, yet the evils of overcrowding, especially in London, were still a public scandal, and were becoming, in certain localities, more serious than they ever were; second, that there was much legislation designed to meet these evils, yet that the existing laws were not put into force.

The condition of the houses themselves was also publicly exposed:

> There can be no doubt but that houses are often built of the commonest materials, and with the worst workmanship, and are altogether unfit for the people to live in, especially if they are a little rough in their ways. The old houses are rotten from age and neglect. The new houses aften commence where the old ones leave off, and are rotten from the first. It is quite certain that the working classes are largely housed in dwellings which would be unsuitable even if they were not overcrowded.

The Commission took evidence from the London Trades Council which included a vitally important principle, already quoted in Chapter 2:

> It is totally impossible that private enterprise, philanthropy and charity can ever keep pace with the present demands. ... Economic forces and population have outstepped their endeavours: hence evils accrue. But what the individual cannot do the state municipality must seek to accomplish ... for it alone possesses the necessary power and wealth.

Housing was thus to be developed from top down; and that influenced housing in this country in a fundamental way.

The report of the Royal Commission resulted in the Housing of the Working Classes Act of 1885 which accepted the necessity for major state intervention in housing. Meantime the crisis of health and sanitation had been confronted by the Public Health Act of 1875. Like its 1848 predecessor it became a landmark in the history of English sanitary institutions.

The Act of Consolidating and Amending the Acts relating to Public Health in England (as it was called in full) gave local authorities powers to control the conditions of their district. The powers were permissive not mandatory. Authorities were encouraged to enforce the Bakehouse Regulation Act, soon to be replaced by the Factory and Workshop Act of 1878, the Artisans and Labourers Dwellings Act of 1875, the Baths and Wash-Houses Act and the Labouring Classes Lodging Act.

The sanitary provisions were wide ranging and effective. Sewers were to be well maintained and replaced with new ones where necessary. House owners were required to connect their drains with the sewer, or if the distance was too great to discharge them into a cesspool. Each new house was to have a proper privy, even if there was some disagreement as to what that was.

Authorities were exhorted to clean the streets and to provide an adequate water supply. New cellar dwellings were prohibited, and those already in existence had to comply with new stipulations. Strict regulations were imposed on lodging houses.

But the most definitive provision, in terms of housing design, was this: Section 157 of the Act empowered local authorities to make by-laws governing the layout of streets and the construction of new buildings—their spatial and sanitary provisions. A 'new house' was said to include, 'the re-erecting of a building pulled down to, or below, the ground floor, or of any frame building of which only the framework is left down to the ground floor, or the conversion into a dwelling house of any building not originally such, or the conversion of one dwelling house into more than one, of a building originally constructed as one dwelling house only'.

The Public Health Act gave local authorities permission to act:

One: with respect to the level, width and construction of new streets and the provision for the sewerage thereof. Two: with respect to the structure of walls, foundations, roofs and chimneys of new buildings for securing stability and the prevention of fires, and for the purposes of fires, and for the purposes of health. Three: with respect to the sufficiency of space about buildings to secure a free circulation of air, and with respect to the ventilation of buildings. Four: with respect to drainage of buildings to water-closets, earth closets, privies, ashpits and cesspools in connection with buildings, and to the closing of buildings or parts of buildings unfit for human habitation and to prohibition of their use of such habitation.

Minimum widths of roads were established: roads were to be at least 24 feet at the front and 15 feet at the back. Minimum cubic contents of rooms were also specified. Unfortunately, since building costs tended to be less if the room was almost a cube, ceilings were often too high and floor areas too small.

To ensure the observance of by-laws, authorities were exhorted to give notice of their intentions and authorised to carry out inspections. They could also pull down any buildings which failed to comply with the by-laws.

In terms of space around the building the Act stipulated:

Every person who shall erect a new domestic building shall provide in front of such a building an open space, which shall be free from any erection thereon above the level of the ground, except any portico, porch, step or other like projection from such building, or any gate, fence or wall, not exceeding seven feet in height.

The clause aimed to prevent building on back land and avoid the unhealthy and crowded narrow courts with houses too close together. Space was as essential, said the Act, at the back as at the front:

Every person who shall erect a new domestic building shall provide in the rear of such building an open space exclusively belonging to such building, and of an aggregate extent of not less than one hundred and fifty square feet, and free from any erection thereon above the level of the ground, except a watercloset, earth closet, or privy and an ashpit.

The Model By-laws were received with mixed feelings. The general principle was good, for action against insanitary conditions and back-to-back houses was long overdue. But what came to be known as 'by-law housing' tended to be dull and uniform—dutifully following the regulations, but unvaried and unimaginative.

It commonly consisted of monotonous terraces of four, six or more houses in long, parallel, treeless streets. The houses had passages leading to walled back yards with a privy and sometimes a coal house. The doors opened directly onto the street.

They were basically through terrace houses with 'a tunnel back' instead of the old 'back-to-back'. Usually built on a grid pattern in long straight lines which followed the minimum dimensions, they were criticised for their monotony and shoddy workmanship.

In appearance, by-law housing was the antithesis of all that Unwin championed. He accepted that 'a certain minimum standard of air-space, light and ventilation has been secured', but deplored the unpleasant appearance of the buildings which seemed to go hand in hand with these otherwise welcome reforms:

> The remarkable fact remains that there are growing up around all our big towns vast districts, under these very by-laws, which for dreariness and sheer ugliness it is difficult to match anywhere, and compared with which, many of the old unhealthy slums are, from the point of view of picturesqueness and beauty, infinitely more attractive.... We have in a certain niggardly way done what needed doing, but much that we have done has lacked the insight of imagination.

By-law regulations had other defects as well as ugliness. For one thing, they were geographically inconsistent, some authorities having no by-laws and others not enforcing those they had. But the by-law housing was superior to anything that had gone before. The houses were at least healthy, adequately exposed to air and moderately exposed to light. They were better insulated from cold, damp and noise, and better ventilated, than earlier buildings. Staircases were less precipitately steep, timber flooring was beginning to replace stone flags, and there was a greater provision of sinks, coppers and cooking ranges. Monotonous they undoubtedly were.

What altered the situation was a movement brought about by two events during and immediately after the Great War. In 1917 the Local Government Board set up, with a view to post-war planning, a committee to consider questions of building construction of dwellings for the working classes. It was chaired by Sir John Tudor Walters, MP. Raymond Unwin was one of its members.

The Tudor Walters Report, published in 1918, was intended to 'profoundly influence the general standard of housing in this country'. Its proposals were revolutionary, initiating a major innovation in social policy, and ultimately affecting the character of working class life. They were to remain a model throughout the inter-war years, and indirectly much longer.

On its appearance in November 1918, the document was recognised as 'the most practical and useful contribution to the housing question published in recent years'. Running to just under 100 pages, the Tudor Walters Report was the first comprehensive treatise on the political, technical and practical issues involved in the design of the small house. In the housing debates of 1918–19, its authority was virtually unquestionable.

In its introduction the Report recognised the gravity of the housing question:

> It is quite evident to those who have examined the facts of the case that special remedies are needed to deal with the acute housing difficulties that have arisen. ... It seems evident from these circumstances that, unless there is some supreme guiding direction, an adequate housing programme is not likely to be carried out, but that the shortage of houses for some years after the war will increase rather than diminish.

The Report proposed reforms in housing policy and administration. It recommended that future house building should be regulated by town-planning schemes instead of rigid by-laws. It also discussed the format of housing programmes, and drew up procedures for site planning and development.

The Report then dealt with the house itself—its standard layout and principles of design. It suggested that the standard house should be a two-storey dwelling with not less than three bedrooms. It also considered the cost and availability of materials, as well as constructive ways of economising. It argued that good economy demanded an improvement in standards. In an implicit criticism of by-law building it showed that savings were made through high not low quality work. It was poor economy to build houses to anything but the highest standards; otherwise, before the loan period had expired, the house would be unlettable.

> In the face of an improving standard it is only wise economy to build dwellings which, so far as may be judged, will continue to be above the accepted minimum. ... to add to the already large supply of houses on the margin line might prove anything but economical in the long run.

Not surprisingly, since Unwin was a member of the committee, Tudor Walters advocated the principle of not more than 12 houses to the acre (eight in the country). It stipulated that the maximum length of a terrace should be eight houses and that there should be a variety of types—an obvious rejection of by-law uniformity.

The importance of beauty was stressed:

> by so planning the lines of the roads and disposing the places and buildings as to develop the beauty of vista, arrangement and proportion,

> an attractiveness may be added to the dwellings at little or no extra cost, which we consider should not only not be omitted, but should be regarded as essential to true economy.

The Report proposed a wider fronted house, in contrast to the narrow by-law frontages, with a 'through' living room to allow maximum air and sunlight:

> The increased frontage on both sides gives better opportunity for lighting and ventilating thoroughly in all parts of the house ... medical opinion is unanimous in allowing plenty of sunshine to penetrate into the rooms.

Another emphasis reminiscent of Unwin was on simplicity of design:

> simple straightforward plans will usually prove most economical ... ornament is usually out of place and necessarily costly both in execution and upkeep.

The Committee emphasised that a third living room was a reasonable and proper expectation and that a house with a parlour was 'undoubtedly the type desired by the majority of the artisan class'. In the event about 40 per cent of post-war local authority houses contained parlours.

The Tudor Walters Report was sensitive and all-embracing, and at the same time responsible. It displayed an informed awareness of rising building costs and the lack of skilled labour. It was also, in many ways, ahead of its time. Some of its proposals, such as heating houses with waste heat from power stations, developing interchangeable building components and increasing by-law flexibility, were as progressive as was its basic reasoning.

The body responsible for implementing the Report's recommendations was the Local Government Board, which was in charge of housing before the Ministry of Health was created. In 1919 the Board issued a *Housing Manual* in which the conditions of government grants were set out. It adopted the main features and proposals of the Tudor Walters Report, but extended the space recommendations.

The *Manual* laid down that every house was to have an internal WC positioned off the back lobby, as well as a bath in either a bathroom or the scullery. Like the Tudor Walters Report, the *Manual* insisted that new housing should 'mark an advance on the building and development which has ordinarily been regarded as sufficient in the past.'

The *Manual*'s emphasis on physical beauty in layout shows again the influence of Unwin:

> By so planning the lines of the roads and disposing the spaces and the buildings as to develop the beauty of vista, arrangement and proportion, attractiveness may be added to the dwellings at little or no extra cost. Good exterior design in harmony with the surroundings and adapted to the site should be secured. ... By the choice of suitable local materials, and the adoption of simple lines and good proportion and groupings of buildings, with well-considered variation in design and in the treatment of prominent parts, good appearance may be secured within the limits required by due economy.

It is a sentiment that almost echoes Tudor Walters verbatim.

The Tudor Walters Report was quickly followed by the Housing and Town Planning Act of 1919, usually known as the Addison Act after its author, Dr Christopher Addison, President of the Local Government Board and later the first Minister of Health.

The Addison Act required local authorities to make a survey of the housing needs in their area, and implement building programmes to meet those needs. What had been permissive powers under the Housing Act of 1890 now became mandatory. For the first time local authorities were given clear responsibility for housing provision, as well as financial support from central government. The financial allowances were generous. The authorities' annual liability was limited to a penny rate. Any further losses would be borne by the Treasury.

The subsidy was not viewed as a long-term policy, but only as a temporary expedient created by the war. In practice, housing subsidies in one form or another have been retained ever since by successive governments. Addison also proposed a solution to the difficulty experienced by local authorities in procuring tenders for housing. That was to involve private enterprise—both building contractors and speculative builders—in local authority projects.

The Act established *council housing* as we know it. In effect, the state had taken over responsibility for working class housing, since the local authority contribution was at first minimal. It also set a precedent for the professional design of mass housing, when Addison commissioned a number of architects to submit plans for the guidance of authorities.

The majority of the cottage plans were the work of S B Russell, FRIBA, who attached importance to a clear layout of streets, sunny living rooms, as many bedrooms as possible, a cool place for the larder, easy access to the coal store and an avoidance of rear projections.

The plans were not mandatory and acted only as guidelines. Local authorities were free to design as they wished, provided they adhered to the space and other requirements. Most authorities produced their own plans within their own architects' or engineers' departments; central government was instrumental in setting standards and making suggestions.

The different interpretations of the Act produced a healthy diversity of housing throughout the country. Some of the best 'Addison' houses were, for example, at Short Heath in Wolverhampton. They had through living rooms, large casement windows, a cooking range and fireplace. They also had hot and cold water, a gas copper, WC and coal store and three bedrooms upstairs.

The London County Council proposed in 1919 to build 29 000 dwellings within five years: 8799 were actually built under the Addison Act. The LCC's architects drew up a series of plans which became models for all the cottage estates. Monotony was avoided by combining the cottages with groups of three and five-storey flats. All terraces had secondary access to the back without having to pass through the house. The most common type had four to six cottages in a 'block', rendered more attractive by preserving existing trees and planting new greens and shrubberies.

But there was a further—and more alarming—dimension to the need to build houses at this time. Accumulating evidence had begun to suggest that substandard housing could be as costly in social as in financial terms.

Efforts to increase war production had revealed that four million working weeks a year were lost through sickness caused by environmental conditions. The Royal Commission, appointed to investigate the reasons for industrial unrest, discovered that inadequate housing was the most common cause of disquiet.

Between 1915 and 1918 the need for a greater supply of arms and armaments prompted the government into a substantial programme of house building for munition workers—not only temporary but also permanent housing. Lloyd George said in June 1915: 'Ultimate victory or defeat depends on the supply of munitions.' It was a failure on this front that was partially responsible for the downfall of Asquith's government and the formation of a coalition government in 1915. In this government, Lloyd George became

Minister of Munitions. The War Office had already stated in December 1914 that the increase in the number of workers 'has made the question of accommodation one of vital importance and urgency in the interests, not merely of the workmen, but of the work itself'.

With the end of the war the government faced a further crisis— the demobilisation of five million men from the armed services, together with the release of a similar number from the munitions factories and other war industries. The need for a dynamic house-building campaign to combat unemployment as well as providing houses, assumed a new alarming urgency.

The transition from war to peace was accompanied by evidence of much dissatisfaction among the people. Unrest, strikes, and the presence of demobilised soldiers in the streets recalled parallel instances in Russia and Germany. Much frightened by the Russian Revolution of 1917, the government took a serious view of the dangers in this country. As the Parliamentary Secretary to the Local Government Board said in 1919: 'The money we are going to spend is an insurance against Bolshevism and Revolution.'

Whether or not such fears were justified, the Cabinet was seriously concerned. Almost as soon as the Armistice was signed in 1918, Whitehall received reports of revolutionary feeling in the country. At the end of January 1919, Clydesiders went on strike to campaign for a 40 hour week.

The Conservative Leader and Deputy Prime Minister, Bonar Law, told the Prime Minister: 'Everything depends on beating the strike in the Glasgow area, as if the strikers are successful there the disorder will spread all over the country.'

Walter Long of the Conservative Party expressed the view that there was 'no doubt that we are up against a Bolshevist movement in London, Glasgow and elsewhere'.

'We must be ready', said Dr Addison, 'for the emergencies of peace.' The emergencies of peace were to need handling as carefully as the emergencies of war if disaster was to be averted. That included people's housing. Lloyd George warned the Cabinet that the people had been promised reform time and time again, yet still nothing had been done. He said: 'We must give them the conviction this time that we mean it, and we must give them that conviction quickly. . . . Even if it costs a hundred million pounds, what is that compared to the stability of the state?'

King George V said in 1919 that 'an adequate solution of the housing question is the foundation of all social progress.' Lord Long was more explicit: 'It would be a black crime indeed if these men come back from the horrible waterlogged trenches to something little better than a pig-sty here . . . and would be a negation of all that has been said during the war.'

In the aftermath of the Armistice the government presented a varied programme of social reform, which included unemployment protection, shorter working hours, industrial democracy and land settlement; but the most urgent issue was the great housing need. Lloyd George intended that housing schemes should renew people's faith in the state and show that there was no need for protest and revolution. They were to be 'Homes fit for Heroes'. It may be that the housing built after the war played a significant part in preventing the political and social unrest which shattered other continental countries.

Among the failures of the Addison Act, one of the chief was that local authorities were slow to carry out their proposed programmes. Rising building costs were transferred to the government; the cost of the Addison Act to the taxpayer amounted to almost one pound a week for every house built. Under increasing criticism and in protest at proposed cuts, Addison resigned.

The main failure of the Addison Act was, however, that owing to high building costs it was unable to reach the targets it had set. 500 000 houses were needed; of these 214 000 were sanctioned and only 170 000 were built.

Addison's Act was succeeded in 1923 by the rather more modest Chamberlain Act. This offered government subsidy to local authorities, conditional financial support to private builders and local authority mortgages for those who had saved enough to buy their own homes. Then, in 1924, a third major Housing Act, the Wheatley Act, passed by the Labour government, doubled the subsidies to local authorities.

John Wheatley, the first Labour Minister of Health, hoped that municipal housing would eventually replace private renting as the normal form of tenure for the working class. Whereas the 1923 Act had set a time limit on local authority grants, the 1924 Act intended to establish long-term investment. It increased the repayment period from 20 years to 40. It also set local authorities production targets; subsidy could be withheld if they failed to meet them.

The primary aim of the Wheatley Act was to restore local authorities to their role as the major providers of working class housing, a position from which they had been ousted by the 1923 Chamberlain Act and its encouragement of private enterprise. The subsidies which had been reduced by the 1923 Act were raised again and a long-term housing programme guaranteed. The new Act recognised that the need for housing was even more acute in 1924 than it had been in 1919, and that builders and local authorities needed the assurance of a lengthy building programme.

The Wheatley Act is generally held to be the most successful of the inter-war housing Acts. It produced a total of 508 000 houses, all but 15 000 of which were provided by local authorities.

In London the County Council developed two main house types. The most attractive of these were the 'Cottage Estates' influenced in design by the work of Unwin and his contemporaries. Excellent examples survive in Roehampton and the Docklands. They can be viewed as the forerunner to town development schemes in the 1950s.

Bellingham and Downham in Kent retained the features of the 'garden city', but Becontree, described as 'the largest municipal housing estate in the world', though not a garden suburb, became the prototype of all housing estates. Other developments in the same period, like the St Helier estate at Merton and Morden, and the Watling estate at Hendon, maintained a high standard of building and amenities up to the end of the thirties. The servicing of houses improved; Castelnau estate in the Barnes peninsula had electricity installed in 57 of its houses, for cooking and heating as well as light; in the remainder, gas was provided for cooking and electricity for light.

The other main LCC type was blocks of flats or 'Flatted Estates'. This consisted of five-storey blocks in a modified neo-Georgian style with sash windows; later versions had standard steel casements and plain brick surfaces. The façades were normally more attractive than the interiors.

The Cottage Estates and Flatted Estates represented a new development in LCC housing design. The flats were highly regarded. Each flat had its own bath and WC, a scullery (which was soon to become a kitchen), a larder and a coal store. A dust-chute was provided for each floor.

The average floor area of a flat was larger than before the war, and the height restriction of the blocks to five storeys meant that the LCC flats avoided many of the problems that the high-rise boom was later to encounter. The flats had through ventilation and balcony access. Kitchens were well fitted and equipped.

Seen in the perspective of *all* the houses built in England and Wales between 1919 and 1934, the situation looks different. Out of the 2.5 million new homes only 31 per cent were built by local authorities, and of the 69 per cent built by private enterprise only a quarter of these received a subsidy. The need that had been identified for a large increase in working class housing for rent had not, in short, been met. The largest increase had been not for the benefit of the working man, but for the more affluent 'middle class' range.

The bulk of house building between the wars was, however, in the private sector. Mortgages became more easily available to both professional classes and skilled manual workers.

Owner-occupation more than quadrupled between 1918 and 1938. About 40 per cent of that increase was due to tenants purchasing their rented homes from the landlord. The move from rented to owner-occupied housing was now firmly under way. Ultimately it was to lead to the virtual collapse of the private rented sector.

There was one further development during the thirties in particular that was to affect the general housing scene in a dramatic way. The government's attention became concentrated upon slum clearance. Sir Ernest Simon calculated that there were about one million unfit houses in England and Wales. The Cabinet diverted its consideration to the huge numbers of families still occupying old, decaying and slum property.

Emphasis in housing policy changed from general to special needs, esecially that of 'slum clearance'. The nature and gravity of the problem was ascertained by the collection, as in the Victorian period, of a disturbing amount of evidence. The precise number of unfit dwellings was never exactly agreed upon. Local authority surveys in 1931 suggested 300 000, the Council for Research on House Construction found 50 000 more and the Liberal Party's estimate was four million.

Whatever the exact statistics it was clear that the need was urgent. London had 30 000 basement dwellings, uncomfortably recalling the cellars of the Victorian period. Leeds had 75 000 of the notorious back-to-backs, of which 33 000 were thought to be 'unfit for human habitation'. 'No other civilised country', wrote one observer in 1935, 'has such vast tracts of slumdom. For size and density, foul air and wretchedness, the slums of Britain are in a class

apart.' Only 37 per cent of London families had a house or flat of their own, and a third of London's population had more than three people to two rooms.

The Census of 1931 showed 54 families in London living at seven or more to one room, conditions that had scarcely improved since the nineteenth century. There was a vast number of slum dwellings in Manchester and of back-to-backs in Sheffield, Birmingham and Bradford. The worst of all were the tenements in the poorest part of every town and city, where families lived in one or two rooms of decaying houses sharing one WC and one water tap among, 40 or 50 people.

A disturbing discovery was that modest figures of population increase since 1918 concealed the increase in the percentage of separate families. Between 1921 and 1931 this increase had absorbed the entire output of new homes. There were therefore still not

enough houses for everyone. Moreover, a survey of income revealed that a large proportion of the working class would need subsidising on a permanent basis.

The foundations of modern slum clearances were laid by the Greenwood Act, passed by the Labour government in 1930. That Act introduced an Exchequer subsidy especially for slum clearance. It related the subsidy to the number of people in need. By basing the subsidy on the people rather than the houses, it made the authorities' job easier with regard to families; the subsidy obviously increased with the size of the family concerned. Local authorities were instructed to restrict rents to what 'people could reasonably be expected to pay' and to submit five year slum clearance plans.

Owing to the economic crisis of 1931 and to changes in government, the clearance project did not get properly under way

Quarry Hill, Leeds, where a famous slum clearance scheme of the 1930s rehoused over 3000 people from the former 'Quarry Hill Unhealthy Area'.

until 1933. The Housing Act of that year stated that the government was committed to 'concentrate public effort and money on the clearance and improvement of slum conditions', and that as far as the provision of ordinary working class homes was concerned it would depend upon private enterprise.

The policy of the Wheatley Act was thus completely reversed. Private enterprise again replaced authorities as providers of working class housing. As regards slum clearance, the failure of the 1933 Act was that it did not specify to local authorities what constituted an effective slum clearance programme, or what indeed constituted an unfit dwelling. As a result, many buildings which should have been demolished were overlooked.

By the outbreak of the Second World War about half the officially declared slums had been cleared. Although much more needed to be done, more had been achieved in this programme than in any project since 1890. The government accepted that slum clearance was a continuing process both because houses age and because people's expectations rise. The number of houses repaired and made habitable was 439 000.

Of all the slum clearance schemes, the most famous and internationally recognised was in Leeds. Quarry Hill, at the east end of the Headrow, had been designated as the Quarry Hill Unhealthy Area at the beginning of the century.

In 1934 the area was wholly cleared, and between that year and 1940, a new housing scheme developed. It was prompted by the Reverend Charles Jenkinson, a Christian socialist who became a councillor when Labour came to power in Leeds in 1933.

Quarry Hill was inspired by housing estates in Vienna and Berlin of the twenties and thirties. Dr Alison Ravetz of Leeds Polytechnic wrote of it:

> Nothing was to be spared to make it the most advanced, magnificent and luxurious estate the world had yet seen; a fitting compensation to slum dwellers for years of neglect and an architectural embellishment to the centre of Leeds.

Dr Ravetz pointed out that Quarry Hill, despite its sanitary principles, displayed a lingering Victorian attitude to the poor and their standards and general morals. New tenants were moved from their old accommodation together with their possessions in a 'bug van'. This was left in a de-infestation centre overnight, and the next day the tenants proceeded to the new flats in Quarry Hill.

Below and right Quarry Hill. Innovatory structural and drainage systems featured in a plan for the whole community in the centre of the city. Now it's no more.

The flats were designed in such a way as to enshrine the sanitary principle and prevent re-infestation. As Dr Ravetz said: 'Obviously tenants were not expected to mend their ways.' There was no timber except in the doors, and metal-framed windows were surrounded with concrete. Skirting boards and other traditionally wooden structures were also made from concrete.

On the other hand Quarry Hill had many desirable social and domestic innovations. It had quality fittings and its many amenities included a shopping centre, playgrounds, crèches and a laundry. It had the Garchey system of waste disposal, a radio relay system, lifts to the eight-storey blocks, tennis courts and a community hall.

On a site of 26 acres it had 938 flats housing over 3000 people. The brief laid down that not more than one fifth of the site should be built upon. The rest was open space for gardens, fresh air, playing and relaxation. In the event, only about 18 per cent was built on. Quarry Hill was a show piece of its kind and very popular with its tenants. Yet in 1978, only 40 years after its completion, Quarry Hill was demolished. There were faults in the cladding and foundations; the houses were subject to damp and corrosion; the social buildings were incomplete; the landscape had degenerated.

The fate of Quarry Hill is an apt end to the story of idealism and experiment, a story continually interrupted by political failures in belief and attempts to halt what now seems an inevitable process. It was, at the time, the biggest scheme of public housing in the provinces, and was recognised as a pioneer.

It was followed by local authority housing on a far larger scale—what seemed at first a triumph and is now seen as a disaster. It is to that housing—housing on a mass scale—that we now turn.

CHAPTER FOUR

SOCIAL HOUSING: THE MASS SOLUTION

After the Second World War the inner residential areas of Britain's cities were transformed by the public housing drive.

In 1946, the majority of local authority dwellings were houses. By 1950, the building of flats had begun to increase, though they were still mainly in low blocks. By 1953, 77 per cent of public dwellings approvals were houses, 20 per cent low-rise flats and 3 per cent high-rise flats. The situation changed markedly in the next few years. The proportion of houses in building approvals continued to decline, while high-rise projects increased in height, numbers and importance. By 1960 and 1966, they formed respectively 15 per cent and 26 per cent of construction programmes.

The question that has to be asked about the housing of the fifties, sixties and seventies is: why did we decide to build high buildings in the first place?

The answer is primarily a response to the need for numbers and speed. During the war, as a result of the bombing, more than 200 000 houses had been destroyed and another 3.5 million damaged. Very little routine maintenance had been carried out on the remainder.

In addition, it was thought that at least 750 000 homes were needed for the new households created by post-war marriages and a rising birthrate. The housing situation was, in short, worse than that which had caused alarm in 1918.

Building started quickly. Between 1945 and 1951, 807 000 dwellings were built for local authorities, 180 000 for private owners, and 28 000 for housing associations and government departments. There were also 157 000 prefabricated temporary units put up towards the end of the war and intended to last 10 years. Some of these still exist.

Such numbers were a considerable achievement in the light of the shortage of materials and a building industry still recovering from the war. The Conservative government which took over in 1951 raised the house building targets still further, and achieved them—

300 000 houses were erected in 1953. The government was able to congratulate itself on output even if it paid less attention to quality.

There were other, more idealistic reasons. High-rise housing was already associated for many designers with progress and the expression of a new technological age. It was, wrote two enthusiasts in 1937, 'a housing type peculiar to our own era' as well as 'a solution to the problem of housing'.

High-rise seemed the inevitable expression of the modern movement in architecture. In a series of plans, exhibitions and books in the 1920s, Le Corbusier had argued for the adoption of high-rise housing as the essential building form of the modern city: 'We must create', he declared, 'the mass production spirit.' His imaginative designs for the city of the future included massive slabs of housing in wide, landscaped, open spaces.

This futurist view of high-rise, as both a symbol of modernity and the saviour of the housing crisis, was reinforced by the advertising of the period. Construction firms like Wimpey and Wates used it to present themselves as fast moving, problem-solving concerns. Wimpey advertisements had pictures of 25-storey flats in Glasgow with the caption, 'Wimpey answers the housing problem'.

There is also the fact that architects have always been tempted to build high buildings, even when they were inappropriate. Tower blocks were a part of architectural and municipal prestige—a desire to make a mark on the landscape, to display technical proficiency and to announce the arrival of a new age.

My own conversion to the idea of high flats came from Robert Matthew. Matthew was architect to the London County Council in the crucial years after the Second World War, when its housing policies were being changed and established. He then moved to Edinburgh as Professor of Architecture and, at the same time, set up his own private practice. I worked for him as a kind of personal assistant (what he called the Departmental Registrar) at the university. There he set up a new department of architecture and started a Housing Research Unit.

Matthew assured me that his conviction that housing should go high started not with Le Corbusier, but with Walter Gropius, the founder of the Bauhaus, and author of one of the definitive texts on modern architecture: *The New Architecture and the Bauhaus* (1936).

Gropius had studied how to obtain the best possible living conditions while maintaining the urban character of the city. His solution was to build high slab-like apartment blocks of about 10 storeys. In two diagrams he showed (a) that at a fixed angle for light between the blocks of 30 degrees, the number of bed spaces (and therefore the number of inhabitants) could be increased by about 40 per cent, and (b) that if the bed spaces were kept to their original number, the angle of light between the blocks could be lowered from 30 degrees to 17.5 degrees. In short, the higher the blocks the greater the space and the better the sunlight. There could be cross ventilation and a great deal of natural light. The idea of the 'verdant city' was, he said, a practical possibility.

A tantalising speculation for me has been whether the housing in this country (profoundly influenced by the LCC's work which was famous throughout Europe) would have been the same if Matthew had not been born and educated in a Scottish city.

For some reason, the Scots have always managed to live in high buildings, one family on top of another, while the English have preferred to stay near the ground in cottages. There are, in fact, good reasons for building high in Scotland. The stone is a good structural material and houses are warmer if they are piled up closely together. On the other hand, the French can live in high flats in a warmer climate; perhaps the Auld Alliance of the Scots and the French had more than a political significance—and reflected a deep psychological identification.

Matthew greatly admired the Edinburgh tenements. I lived in one for some years and then bought two rooms in another when I married. There is nothing fundamentally wrong with living in a flat, in either a high or a low building. What high-rise housing will not suffice for in England and Wales is a family.

To return to the question: why did we build high? It must first be said that in fact the number of high-rise blocks was never in the majority. Of all local authority housing only 6.5 per cent is in high-rise blocks. It just *looks* as if there is more; the image of the modern city can be one of masses of high blocks.

The high-rise blocks were in fact only put up for a period of about 20 years—from roughly the early fifties to the early seventies. By the mid-seventies local authorities were not building any more.

But why were they desirable in the early fifties? It was not because of demand from the prospective tenants, although the top flats quickly became very popular when they were first opened.

69

Highpoint, Highgate, London. The most celebrated
pioneer modern housing scheme in Britain, designed by
Berthold Lubetkin

Nor were they the outcome of sociological study. In the early fifties sociological studies were generally still at a relatively immature stage—and sociological research into housing had hardly started. I remember taking part in interviews to find a sociologist to join the Housing Research team in Edinburgh University in the mid-fifties. Most candidates had no suggestions to offer. The most experienced man suggested that we should put up some housing and he would return in 20 years to say what we had done wrong.

The housing of the fifties and sixties was not the product of theoretical studies; it was essentially a pragmatic solution to definable problems. To the professionals trying to find a way through them, two of these problems were fundamental: the shortage of land, especially where planning policies were limiting the growth of the city outwards; and the overwhelming demand for accommodation. In one city, for example, the new City Architect in the mid-sixties noted that, while his department was building about 2000 houses a year, the application list for houses was 60 000. Any possible answer must include high buildings on limited sites and almost certainly 'system building' for speed. To that I shall return later.

The most basic text, used by the architects of many authorities, was the *County of London Plan* (1943) by Abercrombie and Forshaw. The authors included a number of detailed studies that suggested that at a density of some 135 people per acre it would be possible not only to provide 'improved living conditions for the differing income groups', but vastly superior facilities and adequate open space for health and recreation. In a mixed development of different housing types, some blocks would go high, others could stay nearer the ground. It was a practical, carefully considered solution; but it opened up some exciting possibilities.

The initial enthusiasm for flats and high buildings came mainly from the architects. Two pre-war projects had captured the imagination of the younger members of the architectural profession. In 1933, Wells Coates, a pioneer of modern architecture in England, built the Isokon flats (the Lawn Road flats in Hampstead). It was a concrete building, not very high, with continuous balcony fronts.

Berthold Lubetkin, a Russian émigré who had studied in Moscow, Leningrad and Paris, and was the architect for the famous penguin pool in London Zoo, designed the new apartment blocks in Highgate—Highpoint 1 and Highpoint 2. Highpoint 1 was built between 1933 and 1935, and Highpoint 2 between 1936 and 1938.

Highpoint 2 (*previous page*) has a porch supported by Greek maidens, the Caryatids. Highpoint 1 (*below*) is pure modern. Berthold Lubetkin (*right*) thinking about the future of modern architecture and very serious.

They were eight-storey blocks with individual balconies. Highpoint 2 has an entrance canopy supported by replicas of Greek goddesses— the Caryatids of Athens.

Both blocks are very attractive and were quickly popular. Talking to me in 1988, Lubetkin, then 88 years old, had no doubt about the soundness of the decision.

In answer to my question: What is the essence of the modern movement as you understood it in the 1920s and the 1930s?, he replied: 'Glorifying reason in human affairs, getting rid of prejudice and facing reality as it is.' Why then, I asked, did you have to build high? In reply he pointed out that you can't take a design and find an exact cause for everything you see in it; they are inter-connected. 'Highpoint had to accommodate a certain amount of people on a restricted site, and that in itself dictated the height of it. But apart from that,' he continued, 'there was the emotional impact of a white thing, standing on top of the cliffs, and waiting for the winds of

change to come.' It was a romantic vision; utility and imagination were to go hand in hand.

The illogicality of applying such an approach to local authority housing was this: high buildings are suitable—and may even be the best kind of dwelling—for the well-to-do. They are costly to construct and need much care and maintenance. Ideally, they need staff to control them and to ensure, at the very least, that the lifts work. The mistake was to apply this to housing for the ordinary working man—houses promoted and maintained by local authorities, always short of money, always trying to economise.

Highpoint, after all, was built to very high standards. It had not only ordinary passenger lifts, but service lifts. There were specially designed switches on the metal door frames, the taps were new. On the roof there was a terrace worthy of Le Corbusier, with a wonderful view over London. Le Corbusier himself visited the block, and called it 'a vertical garden city'.

73

Local authority housing was subject to a different series of constraints. As far as the dwellings themselves were concerned, the most influential document was a report on the design of dwellings produced by the Ministry of Health Central Housing Advisory Committee in 1944. The chairman of the committee was the Earl of Dudley.

All the major recommendations of the Dudley Report were embodied in *The Housing Manual*, published in the same year. The Dudley Report drew attention to two main defects in pre-war council housing. They were the lack of variety in housing types and insufficient living space. The key to their planning would rest upon attention to the kitchens.

Three types of house plan emerged from the study, each of which was to influence council housing for many years to come. The first was a living room combined with a kitchen, with a small scullery nearby. The second was a large living room combined with a dining room, and a working kitchen. The third was for an ordinary living room and a combined dining kitchen; that, of course, involved a separate utility room for washing etc. It was expected that heating would be by gas or electricity rather than by solid fuel. The question of whether there should be a separate parlour, a matter which had been discussed continuously in the inter-war period, still remained a matter for speculation, but in due course the separate parlour disappeared. There would be higher standards of servicing and equipment—houses should contain refrigeration and for families of five or more there should be two WCs; this practice was started in 1945 but abandoned in 1951.

The Dudley Report represented a considerable advance on the Tudor Walters Report which had influenced housing after 1918. The density of housing, confirmed in the subsequent *Housing Manual*, would vary between 30 people per acre and 120 people per acre. In terms of layout, what came to be accepted as a result of the Reports and the continued studies thereafter, was 'mixed development'.

One of the first examples of planned mixed development was the Somerford Estate, built 1947–9, designed for Hackney Borough Council by Frederick Gibberd, the architect for Harlow New Town. But the authority that exploited mixed development in the most remarkable manner was the London County Council—the first authority, incidentally, to employ a sociologist to advise on housing.

In order to expedite the huge housing programme after the war in 1945, the LCC had created an organisation under the Director of Housing and Valuer. In a traumatic reorganisation soon after his arrival, Robert Matthew insisted on having housing transferred to the Architects Department, where it seemed most naturally to belong. After all, architects were trained to design for people; they should therefore be responsible for housing, the biggest programme of work in building. Whether or not, in the event, that was the right decision, for the time being it led to some of the most celebrated housing in the world.

The LCC set up a Housing Division and rapidly built up a Housing Development Group, recruiting bright young architects from schools of architecture and the more progressive authorities like Hertfordshire.

The first LCC development of the new kind was at Akroydon. But the most complete and expressive scheme, which architects came from many parts of the world to study and admire, was at Roehampton, on the edge of Richmond Park.

Nearby was one of the best of the early LCC Cottage Estates, completed in 1927. Now, with a mature landscape, Roehampton offered an unusual opportunity—it was more or less an approximation to a garden city setting.

Every tree possible was saved. The designers drew up a detailed plan of the site, including each individual tree, to ensure the minimum possible damage. The views to and from the blocks were carefully considered.

But above all, Roehampton was the prime example of mixed development. In pursuit of that ideal, the LCC evolved a concept of housing unlike anything on the Continent. Instead of huge blocks or repetitive rows of low density housing, a mixed development would have a combination of diverse dwellings suited to the requirements of diverse people. It would include single-storey cottages for the elderly, two or three-storey terraced houses for families and a proportion of flats in higher blocks, mainly for childless and elderly couples. At a density of about 120 people to the acre this would still allow ample room for landscape, for play and exercise. Mixed development, therefore, would produce some of the best of both low and high density housing.

Roehampton was built in two phases—first the Alton Estate in Portsmouth Road, and then the Alton Estate in Clarence Avenue. The first scheme, with its point blocks and low housing, was distinctly

Scandinavian in character. The architects had studied Scandinavian housing at first hand and were convinced that it was appropriate. Groups of 11-storey point blocks were sited among the trees, five-storey slab blocks were surrounded by a stretch of meadow, there were terraced houses and four-storey maisonettes on the narrower parts of the plot.

The second Alton Estate, the later and bigger development, was designed by the new wave of keen young architects in the Department, devotees of Le Corbusier and of his Unité d'Habitation at Marseille. This took the form of slab blocks with balcony access, later very unpopular, and rough concrete, later more unpopular still.

But the other housing types were still there—the point blocks, the four-storey maisonettes, the two-storey terraced houses and the single-storey houses for old people. The total environment was incomparable. Its major fault, very visible today, is the lack of space for car parking; at the time it was not anticipated that car ownership would increase to the level it has today.

As an estate Roehampton has not diminished in popularity. There are, of course, variations in the popularity of different types of block. Tower blocks remain popular, as do two-storey houses. The least popular are the four-storey maisonettes and the slab blocks. But the findings of Roehampton did not in the end influence the general pattern of housing in the country. In other parts of London, densities were increased to 200 people per acre and more. In many parts of the country, the most successful and popular dwelling types, for the time being at least, were the tower blocks. In 1988 there were 429 tower blocks in Birmingham alone. Great Britain could boast 4600 such blocks.

High-rise housing was popular not only with architects, but with local councillors and their officials—especially the borough engineers. As Berthold Lubetkin pointed out to me, the argument of the borough engineer was that the cost of drainage and bringing in services could be solved by concentrating the whole project. Fewer roads were needed. Furthermore, the high buildings were not of traditional construction in the main, but were constructed through the adoption of *system building*. The major advantage was speed—both in the acquisition of land for a tower block and in the construction process using a prefabricated system. Contracting organisations vied with each other in producing systems. The long-term results of these are now with us.

The LCC's Alton Estates at Roehampton set a new standard in post-war housing, providing for young and old.

The LCC pioneered 'mixed development', with point blocks, slab blocks, 4-storey maisonettes, terraces and single-storey houses – to accommodate different family sizes and ages. Very successful and still popular.

Point blocks on the second phase at Roehampton, set in the mature landscape, much influenced in style by Le Corbusier.

For the time being, central government encouraged, by advice and grants, the use of such systems. To achieve housing targets quickly, it seemed that something more than traditional construction was needed. Non-traditional techniques were recommended—steel frames, timber frames, and especially concrete. The need for speed and mass accommodation was thus a primary cause for the building of high blocks of flats using prefabricated techniques. To build high-rise housing satisfied the need for quicker results and greater numbers, and high densities involved the use of less land than traditional low-rise housing.

But above all, high-rise housing was advocated and supported by central government. Local authorities were urged, through circulars, to build high. It was clear that building high must cost more per square foot than building a traditional two-storey house. Central government, therefore, supplied grants for building high. Everyone, it seemed, would be happy. The houses went up quickly, the politicians could congratulate themselves, the builders made fabulous profits. A few authorities might refuse to build high-rise housing—the chairman of York's Housing Committee, for example, refused to have anything to do with it—but generally the subsidies, the encouragement and the speed provided local authorities with the illusion of a great achievement.

So what went wrong? How and why did public attitudes change?

First there was the problem of children. Surveys in the late 1950s indicated that while many single people and childless couples liked living in flats, the majority of families with children disliked them. As early as the 1890s T C Horsfall had said that 'children shouldn't live in flats'.

Ernest Dove, a resident of a 14-storey tower block, supported this view many years later: 'I think it's all wrong that young children should live in flats ... they have nowhere to play.' In similar vein, Phyllis Simon, another 14-storey tenant, said: 'When they [children] get in these flats it's like prisons. These flats are alright for couples, older couples, those without kids.' (Allaun, 1972). One mother was decidedly more scathing: 'The architect who designed this flat ought to be forced to live in it for six months.' Parents voiced fears that children might fall from windows or be damaged by lifts. In addition to this, there was evidence that life in a high flat might adversely affect children both physically and psychologically.

Such an environment could be no less damaging to mothers, who felt cut off and lonely living in high-rise blocks. The removal of families to peripheral estates, often as a result of slum clearance, also broke up the community and destroyed the extended family.

Other dissatisfactions felt by high-rise tenants were noise, the high incidence of crime and vandalism, and especially the frequent failure of lifts. One resident recalled: 'My married daughter came one lunchtime and was trapped in a lift for over half an hour. She became hysterical. ... It's a terrible sensation to be locked in a lift. I've been locked in it several times myself.'

In housing schemes, there was usually no social plan equivalent to the physical plan. Everyone was in too much of a hurry—and in any case the architects, concerned with numbers and densities and the design of the environment, had enough to deal with. Their confidence was sometimes breathtaking.

Nicholas Taylor, formerly assistant editor of the *Architectural Review*, recalled:

> In 1967 ... I was asked by my editor to put together a special issue ... which would illustrate 'the best of current housing design' together with a text explaining 'what should be done'. ... My idea of importing into the argument some sociological evidence of what ordinary people actually wanted was scornfully dismissed by the proprietor, De Cronin Hastings, with the words 'But we KNOW what should be done'.

In fact, many architects at the time of the tower block boom did express a concern for the social context. But it was usually accepted that concern should yield to the pragmatic. Yamasaki, the respected American architect, designer of the now notorious Pruitt–Igoe scheme in St Louis, wrote: 'As an architect, if I had no economic ... limitations, I'd solve all my problems with one storey buildings. ... Yet we know that within the framework of our present cities this is impossible to achieve.'

But information about social conditions and social needs could not be indefinitely ignored. The Metropolitan Borough of Fulham, while welcoming redevelopment, attacked the policy: 'For our part we consider that the primary purpose of planning control is to resist blind economic pressures and recognise social needs.' Some housing managers, committed to high-rise buildings, admitted that 80 per cent of their tenants would prefer to live in houses. But no authority except the LCC appears to have had any real procedure for assessing tenants' reaction to their dwellings.

A disastrous event in May 1968 brought a final climax to the growing dissatisfaction with high-rise flats. An elderly lady on the sixteenth floor of the Ronan Point flats in London, lit her gas early one morning. There was an explosion, the load bearing walls of her flat blew out, and the phenomenon known as progressive collapse took place.

The living rooms of all the flats in one corner of the block collapsed on top of each other, together with all the bedrooms above the sixteenth floor. Five people were killed and 17 injured. Most people were still in bed; had they not been, the death toll would have been heavier.

An inquiry was immediately launched into the Ronan Point disaster. After much delay, the report showed that the building structure had merely followed national trends, which proved to have been inadequately researched.

83

Checking for faults in the high-rise blocks. Birmingham City Council finds it simpler and better to employ teams to abseil down the blocks and record any faults.

The Ronan Point tragedy caused an overdue decline of high-rise in public and professional opinion. Architects who had been some of its most stalwart supporters now spoke out increasingly against it. In an article in the *Architectural Review*, entitled 'The Failure of Housing', Nicholas Taylor complained: 'More slums are likely to be built in the next five years than in the next twenty.'

This opinion was confirmed by later developments. Some tower blocks became so unpopular it was hard to find people to live in them. In 1979, the first block of unlettable flats was demolished by Birkenhead District Council, just over 20 years after their completion. Liverpool was facing similar difficulties with the flats nicknamed 'The Piggeries'.

There were further revelations. The growing disillusionment of architects with the inherent weaknesses and substandard quality of high-rise housing went hand in hand with doubts as to whether there were any significant savings in either land or building costs. National data on building costs showed that in 1960 all forms of high-rise were more than twice as expensive per square foot as three-bedroomed houses. Even the alleged cheapness of high densities was a myth, as Unwin had perceived years before. Moreover, land was more costly in the inner cities, where the majority of tower blocks were built. And, despite the high price of flats, their quality was often poor. One of the problems of the 1970s was the large stock of dwellings which were expensive to build, but technically and socially deficient.

A survey by Birmingham City Council's Housing Department showed that nearly all the Council's 429 tower blocks, though not in danger of collapse, were perilously shedding their cladding of brick and concrete. Apart from the physical danger, expensive repairs had to be carried out.

There were still further disadvantages. High-rise had often been favoured for its putative quickness of construction. Yet this too was a myth. In the short term it might be a quick solution to the housing crisis. Within the complex timescale of public housing, however, one construction scheme was generally no swifter than another. Houses on the ground could be occupied as soon as each was complete; with high-rise the whole block—40 to 80 or more dwellings—had to be finished before any could be occupied. In fact, in the industrialised building programme, completion times for public authority flats were longer than for other housing types.

In 1969, Desmond Plummer, leader of the GLC, declared: 'The

85

Government pressurised us into erecting these types of system built flats to save time and money.' Realising, however, that they were actually saving on neither, the government became less and less willing to encourage high-rise building. Restrictive densities for public housing were imposed. Tower blocks came to be disqualified for government subsidy and loan sanction approval.

By 1970, ministry policy had came round to a firmly anti-high-rise position. Cost controls were enforced which effectively eliminated high-rise and high-density public housing developments. The planning assumptions which had produced and dominated high-rise were questioned and partially revised. The Department of the Environment limited new housing to a density range of 70 to 100 rooms per acre, with housing for families 'normally in the lower part of the range'.

High densities would only be acceptable either where the number of family dwellings in any given scheme was small and could be provided primarily in low-rise building, or where dwelling houses as distinct from flats or maisonettes were provided. By the end of the 1960s no new high-rise schemes were starting on the drawing boards. But by that time more than 1.5 million people had been rehoused in high flats; not only in London: the mass housing movement had spread to all the big cities. The main projects, which are still there and will be for the indefinite future, were in Glasgow, Leeds, Manchester and Sheffield.

Sheffield can boast the most famous of the schemes. The Gleadless development was a mixed development, very popular with the residents. It was, however, not the most celebrated. Park Hill, built in the early sixties on a slope above the Midland Railway Station, appeared at first to be well liked and very popular with the tenants. Some care was taken to rehouse people, moved as a result of slum clearance, as near to their original home as possible.

The blocks, four storeys at the upper end of the slope and 14 at the lower, were linked and had wide walkways, thought of as the equivalents of the former streets below and given the same names. It was assumed that tenants would use the streets in the air as they had used those on the ground. If this happened at first, there is some doubt that it continued for long.

It certainly did not happen in Hyde Park, the next stage of Sheffield's housing project, built higher up the hill. The flats have badly deteriorated and are considered unsuitable for children. The 1200

Park Hill, Sheffield, famous throughout Europe and visited by architects from many countries. A city on a hill in the city centre, wide streets in the air, the very image of modern living.

dwellings, compactly packed together, are all in need of refurbishment. The concrete is spalling and the waste disposal system needs replacing. Hyde Park is, at the time of writing, being altered to provide accommodation for the International Student Games.

In the late 1960s some architects tried to overcome the disadvantages of high-rise buildings while retaining high densities. These schemes aimed to keep families on or near the ground and to reduce the tall blocks as much as possible. Such schemes as those in Alexandra Road and Maiden Lane in London were very ingenious, with densely packed houses, narrow and tortuous access ways and underground car parking. They have proved disastrous as domestic environments. The remaining open space is too restricted for the children it has to serve, the access ways and car parks are a mugger's paradise and prone to vandalism, and the complexity has produced technical defects.

But ultimately the worst housing to result from the rush to accommodate numbers, with little reference to standards and facilities, was that of the peripheral estates on the edge of the cities.

Panorama of the great architectural dream. Park Hill and Hyde
Park in Sheffield. A total environment, brilliantly ingenious
planning, instant fame, subsequent disillusion.

Glasgow, Easterhouse. Once notorious for its failure both socially and architecturally, now seeing a renaissance through co-operative energy. Architectural transformation.

Notorious examples are Bransholme and Orchard Park outside Hull, and Castlemilk and Easterhouse in Glasgow.

The post-war estates at Bransholme and Orchard Park have maintenance problems brought about by poor insulation and poor materials. Five hundred so-called 'misery maisonettes' have been demolished. Bransholme, in particular, lacks any sense of intimacy. The design is repetitive, the estate is dominated by roads and engineering, the houses are built to low standards with poor heating and insulation and bad condensation.

Orchard Park, another large estate on Hull's outskirts, consists of 3500 dwellings constructed during the 1960s as part of the slum clearance programme. Similar in appearance to Bransholme, it is divided into four 'villages', dominated by 11 multi-storey blocks.

At Castlemilk in Glasgow, where in 1959 it was decided to build 20-storey blocks on the highest part of the scheme, 12 nursery schools, nine primary schools and three secondary schools were planned, together with major social facilities, including eight shopping centres, a cinema, a library and swimming baths. Many years passed before the full quota of schools was completed and the shopping centres still number only five. The community centre and swimming baths have just been provided.

These facilities, however, seem lavish compared with those of Easterhouse. At Easterhouse, the authorities built what was effectively a new town of nearly 50 000 people in a faceless, unvariegated mass of housing. It lacks the social amenities usually found in a new town, as well as those of an older settlement.

The town centre of Easterhouse has one supermarket and one bank for a population of 50 000. Despite this, most of the residents want to stay in Easterhouse; it is after all their home. There are over 20 active community groups there. One of them—the Calvay Street Cooperative—has acquired the houses, obtained grants and transformed the environment with the help of community architects. The housing manager believes it is a pattern for the future.

In general these vast housing estates, built on farmland on the outskirts of a city, over-populated and under-equipped, could only ever have been a partial solution to the housing problem. They lacked the very facilities that make a community viable. And far from providing remedies, they generated problems of their own.

In what may be seen as a dramatic climax to the story of mass housing, a number of local authorities in and around Yorkshire

Hunslet Grange, Leeds, once the pride of the Yorkshire
Development Group, mass housing with an aggressive brutality,
designed jointly by architects and builders, now totally
demolished.

determined towards the end of the 1960s to develop their own
system of building. The housing of the Yorkshire Development Group
(YDG) was to be designed by a team of architects, but developed and
manufactured by a contractor, thus bringing together the design and
construction expertise of both parties.

Grouped blocks were erected in Leeds, Hull, Sheffield and Manchester. They had balcony access, dramatic chutes for the disposal of
waste, storey-height cladding panels in concrete, with exposed
aggregate, which is usually grey, in Leeds black. It was a disaster,
nowhere more obviously than in Leeds where the YDG blocks of
Hunslet Grange were uninhabitable and had to be demolished. In
Sheffield, the Broomhill flats are due to be demolished in 1989. They
have been empty since 1984.

92

The blocks looked as they do now, dark and menacing to residents and observers; but it was the technical faults that were finally decisive. The sodden walls and squelching floors eventually became intolerable. It will be about 40 years before the costs of building are finally paid off.

The YDG blocks can be seen as a terrible warning, or simply as the terminal effort to find a mass solution to what was thought to be a mass problem, but was, in fact, a huge collection of many smaller problems. In the end, it was not so much high-rise housing that did not work; it was mass housing.

Today, the shape of housing policy looks very different from that of the years of the high-rise boom. Few, if any, high flats are being built in the public sector. Neo-vernacular building using traditional materials dominates the local authority output of houses and low-rise flats.

The question that remains about high-rise and mass housing, after more than 30 years of development and disaster, is this: is it possible to transform or reorganise the unsuccessful mass housing so as to make it a positive force in social architecture?

In any housing situation, the crucial factors are design, management and maintenance. All three factors have been partial failures. So, given a poor design, is it possible to redeem the housing through better management and maintenance? An increasing number of experiments suggest that the answer is positive. The key to it, in every case, has been giving the people in a housing scheme authority over their own area—to help them to participate in the formation of a community, responsible for the management and maintenance of their dwellings.

In Manchester, for example, housing estates such as Hulme are thought to be among the worst in the country. Through discussion with tenants, the authorities are in some cases successfully transforming the administration of formerly unmanageable properties. Tenant consultation is to play a key role in future policies. Housing officers admit that quick solutions without the co-operation of the tenants have always failed in the past. Manchester, like many other authorities, is recognising that the most productive way to reform housing and promote good relations is by reference to those who actually live in it.

A positive instance of tenant and council communication in Manchester is the Miles Platting estate. Miles Platting has a Housing

Action Team working together to solve its problems. The top storeys of maisonettes have been removed to create traditional houses; these have been given front and back gardens, car parking spaces, high fences and protection against graffiti. All this has happened after consultation with the tenants, who should after all be best equipped to know what the estate needs. Before the project started, only 14 per cent of residents wanted to stay on the estate; now 80 per cent want to remain.

In Newcastle, the Ryehill estate is to be refurbished. Plans for this were made in conjunction with the Tenants Association, which has been active for two and a half years. Tenants, when consulted in this way, tend to look at the wider implications of what they want—with constructive consequences. The Bingham estate on the outskirts of Edinburgh was deteriorating and had to be demolished. In 1984, the Labour council drew up a design brief for its reconstruction, with extensive co-operation from the tenants.

An important recent feature in the development of high-rise housing has been the conversion of some blocks into homes for the elderly. In Birmingham, where two-thirds of the housing demand in the city is for single person accommodation, both for the young and the elderly, the council accepts that the targeting of specific blocks for specific social groups, reminiscent of the ethos behind mixed development, is fruitful.

So 54 blocks have been transformed since 1979 into sheltered housing for the elderly, with wardens in residence. Following the success of these blocks, more are now in the pipeline. The conversion involves gutting a ground-floor flat to create a community area, installing an intercom service throughout, and employing a permanent warden for each block. It is proving a very effective scheme; residents have no doubt that a community is being formed.

The evidence shows that the elderly who were already living in high-rise flats almost unanimously welcome the transformation of tower blocks, and regard such work as an improvement in their living conditions. Those who are moved there from traditional houses are less enthusiastic. Most people prefer a house, and tend to look upon flats as a temporary mode of dwelling.

A crucial element in making tower blocks pleasanter places to live in is the appointment of a caretaker or *concierge*. Gloucester House in Kilburn has been given a new lease of life by its *concierge* Sharon Coudy, aided by her husband Colin. Where there used to be graffiti, frequent break-ins, and lifts out of action, there have been, since Sharon's arrival, no break-ins, and the lifts operate effectively. Her employment was suggested by the residents themselves.

Everybody joins the Tenants Association in Gloucester House upon moving into the estate. It organises trips for the elderly, and at Christmas and Easter gives each child a present paid for out of proceeds from raffles and jumble sales. The block, from being a rundown dwelling where no one wanted to live, is now described as 'a popular choice for tenants'.

The judges of the London Housing Unit's Tenants' Choice Awards praised the scheme for what it had achieved at relatively little cost. A report by the council comparing Gloucester House with another block, Hereford House, that has no reception system, convinced the council of the financial benefits of the project, as well as the tenant satisfaction which resulted.

Looking back at the story of mass housing, it has to be said that high-rise housing was not merely the product of architectural egotism or of an artistic and technological dream. It was thought to be a real answer to very pressing housing problems, and a genuine step forward in dwelling standards, especially compared with the slums from which many high-rise occupants were rehoused.

The problem was that the reality did not fulfil the dream. The numbers game subsumed everything else. The urgent need for fast rebuilding meant that many of the projected amenities never came into existence. Nor were the structural methods properly researched, especially by local authorities.

Kenneth Campbell, head of LCC and GLC housing between 1959 and 1974, attributed the failure of high-rise housing to three basic faults: first, the inadequate state of the lifts, which were constructed too cheaply; secondly, young couples who moved into tower blocks could not always be moved out again as soon as they had children; thirdly, the size of the Director of Housing's organisation meant that management and maintenance were slow-working, often with unfortunate consequences. If lifts and security worked and could be guaranteed, the story would be very different.

In fact, high-rise has never been universally unpopular. Many childless couples and wealthier people positively like them. Wealthy people, in particular, often enjoy living in high buildings, especially if they have another house in the country. It is in the public sector that high-rise is most resented. The chief problems of the tower blocks—alienation, vandalism and crime—are the result of mass, rather than high-rise housing.

Yet high-rise housing did make some useful contributions. It pinpointed the need for more sensitive slum clearance so that people could be rehoused as near as possible to their original homes, thus keeping communities together. Park Hill, in Sheffield, was well liked primarily because it succeeded in doing this.

Ultimately it highlighted the necessity of having a sociological basis for housing, and for consulting people about what they required and what needed to be done. When local authorities and private developers have the power to destroy whole communities and create new ones, with far-reaching human consequences, a concern not only for bricks and mortar, but for people, must be the key to any solution of the housing question. Housing after all is for people.

CHAPTER FIVE

THE END OF THE CONSENSUS

More than 1.5 million people were housed in high-rise blocks, but that represented only about 6.5 per cent of local authority dwellings. Their rise and fall in public estimation—and probably, in the end, literally—is material for drama, possibly for tragedy—a drama of optimism turning into arrogance and ending in disaster.

The general dislike of faceless modern architecture found its main targets in city centre development and high-rise housing—in city centres and on peripheral estates.

In 1967, Duncan Sandys, who as Minister of Housing and Local Government had founded the Civic Trust, landed by chance the right to promote a private member's bill. Under guidance from the Civic Trust he launched the Civil Amenities Act.

The Town Planning Act which followed in 1968 confirmed the policy of designating Conservation Areas. The next year saw the third element in the change to the whole approach of development and housing. That was the Housing Act of 1969. The emphasis changed from clean sweep mass development to smaller groups, and from new building to the rehabilitation of existing stock.

The Housing Act of 1969 gave refurbishment a fresh impetus. More funds were allocated to both discretionary and standard improvement grants. Another grant set up under this Act was for installing basic amenities in multiple occupied properties. Grants could be used for repairs and replacements, up to one third of the cost of the whole. The Minister could also increase the value of the grant at his discretion in deserving cases; this happened extensively with London claimants. There was increased grant provision for houses of three or more storeys.

The importance of these Acts was this. The 1969 Act was the first to provide an Exchequer subsidy for environmental improvement as well as the improvement of the house itself. The Act altered and extended the existing provision for amendments to an entire area. General Improvement Areas (GIAs) replaced Comprehensive

Development Areas (CDAs). GIAs were areas selected by local authorities which had the potential to be upgraded; places in too advanced a state of disrepair failed to qualify.

And there was a further dimension. Although local authorities were especially urged to look out for GIAs, other non-governmental groups or individuals could recommend them. Under the same scheme Housing Action Areas (HAAs) were established. Their aim was the overall reform of houses, of open space and of landscape.

In the raising of standards, initiatives could now be taken by private individuals and groups as well as by the local authorities. Professionals pooled their resources. Architects, community workers and housing officers began to work together in a corporate attempt to raise standards.

They were further raised by the publication of the Parker Morris Report of 1961. The Tudor Walters Report of 1918 and the Dudley Report of 1944 had both been revolutionary and enormously influential in the development of housing types and housing sizes. The Parker Morris Report was arguably even more progressive: it advocated standards for all new houses, both public and private.

It aimed to keep pace with rising expectations and better postwar conditions. Increased prosperity meant one in three households now owned a car. Two out of three owned a television set. As the Report said: 'These changes in the way people want to live, the things which they own and use, and in their general level of prosperity ... make it timely to re-examine the kinds of homes that we ought to be building.' The Report laid special emphasis on space and on heating. It maintained that the family house should be bigger, that in a house for five or more people there should be two day rooms and two WCs. It recommended a larger kitchen to accommodate the growing range of kitchenware, and a generous amount of storage space.

Better heating was a central stipulation. As most people could only afford to heat one or two rooms during the winter, many rooms were used purely as sleeping areas. The most common form of heating was still the open fire with a back boiler, which could heat only one or two radiators. Parker Morris suggested that houses should be equipped to heat the kitchen and circulation areas to a minimum of 55°F, and living areas to a minimum of 65°F. There should be a system whereby the tenant could regulate the temperature level—and therefore the expense.

In short the Report advocated larger, better planned and better constructed houses than had hitherto been provided. It believed that the higher standard of living ought to be reflected in a higher standard of housing:

> An increasing proportion of people are coming to expect their homes to do more than fulfil the basic requirements. ... There is therefore an increasingly prevalent atmosphere in which improvements in housing standards will be welcomed and indeed demanded, and in which stress will be laid upon quality rather than mere adequacy.

The Report recognised the additional cost involved in the innovations. It therefore suggested that the Parker Morris standards should not be made mandatory but should be adopted gradually. By 1965 only 20 per cent of new council houses had fully adopted the improvements. This slow rate of progress moved the Labour Government to make the recommendations mandatory—for public sector housing in new towns from 1967, and for local authorities from 1969.

The insistence on better standards coincided wtih a new emphasis on rehabilitation rather than whole-scale redevelopment and mass housing. Most authorities responded quickly to the provisions under the 1969 Housing Act. In the forefront of more mixed and pragmatic policies, Birmingham within a few years had cancelled all proposals for four-storey maisonettes and high-rise housing and concentrated instead on policies for restoration and rehabilitation—reducing the height of tall blocks and 'enveloping' existing terrace houses (that is, making the exterior wind and water-tight, renewing roofs, and painting the exterior, while leaving the interiors to the owners).

That was a policy that affected both local authority and private houses. More fundamental and widespread was a major development in the organisation of housing. That was the development of Housing Associations. Though not known originally by that name, Housing Associations date back to the 1830s. The earliest of them, the Society for Improving the Conditions of the Labouring Classes, was originally established as the Labourer's Friend Society in 1830. It began housing work in 1844 and survived until the 1950s, when it was taken over by the Peabody Trust. There were further developments in the 1930s. In Sunderland, for example, groups of buildings known as the Garths were erected to solve problems of unemployment, and also to provide housing which was by that time desperately needed. But now Housing Associations received a major boost. The 1965 Housing

The Garths, Sunderland. One of the most successful of the
Housing Associations of the 1930s.

A community party to celebrate the 50th anniversary of Covent Garden Garth.

The Garths. Unpretentious brick blocks with gallery access and features often deplored nowadays, but actually a very successful community development.

Act set up the Housing Corporation specifically to provide funds for Housing Associations. The Associations were to provide dwellings, either at cost rents, as under the 1961 pilot scheme, or on the basis of group ownership by tenants.

For many years it was complicated and time-consuming to obtain grants from the Housing Corporation. But by the early seventies the process had been speeded up. Moreover, Housing Associations were empowered to borrow more money than before. The ethos of housing moved from quantity to quality. Schemes were smaller than they had been in the early sixties. For several years in the seventies all the housing programmes which received awards were those by Housing Associations—mostly schemes of about 30 to 100 houses.

The particular emphasis on housing was on housing to rent. At a conference in 1965, the Minister of Housing, Richard Crossman, defined the new programme as a bid to 'combat a shortage of one particular kind of housing, namely accommodation to let, at moderate rents to people who could not afford to become owner occupiers'.

Under the 1964 Act a Building Society normally lent two-thirds of the necessary amount, and the Housing Corporation one-third. The Housing Corporation was granted £100 million for its part in the process. By March 1976, it reported that loans had been approved for 43 000 co-ownership dwellings.

But co-ownership was only a part of the achievement of the Housing Associations. They also specialised in the conversion and improvement of old houses. They had begun this work in the inter-war period. In the sixties and seventies, with the accent on restoration, they made it a major part of their achievement. Under the Housing Subsidies Act of 1967 and the Housing Act of 1969, Housing Associations were given a special improvement subsidy—in most cases worth more than the tenant's discretionary grant. They also received more help than before from local authorities. Many authorities lent capital or raised their original grant. The GLC was an especially generous example of this, increasing its funding from £7 million to £25 million a year.

The Housing Finance Act of 1972 extended the lending powers of the Housing Corporation. But the turning point for Housing Associations was the Housing Act of 1974, which for the first time made money available on the right scale. Under the new legislation the Corporation could lend to any Housing Association, not just to those managing cost rent and co-ownership schemes. It also made funds payable through the Department of the Environment—not on request or at the discretion of local authorities as before.

What then is the difference between ordinary private housing, public housing and the Housing Associations?

The difference is one of approach. The voluntary organisations are composed of professionals, motivated partly by public spirit, partly by the chance to give themselves commissions. Their members consist of architects, surveyors, accountants, lawyers and planners. Not surprisingly their standards are higher than those of the local authorities.

Local authorities are required to assess the housing needs of the area and to act upon them: that action is a compulsory part of their function. Private developers build houses for profit. That Housing Associations provide housing at all is a purely voluntary concern. Thus they have been described as 'housing's third arm'. They resemble local authorities in that they build and develop subsidised properties for rent. In this way they supplement council and privately owned housing, giving priority to those with real needs.

Whereas in the 1930s Housing Associations campaigned for social amenities such as nursery schools, and for such items as hot water systems at a time when water was heated in a copper and transferred by a pump to the bath, in the 1950s and 1960s Housing Associations were active in providing specialised accommodation— for example, accommodation for old people. Many local Associations experimented with self-contained flatlets for the elderly, together with an internal warden scheme. In the long term, therefore, the overall contribution of the Associations has been to seek out and meet special needs.

In the 1980s the Housing Associations are very much alive—and possibly about to become larger and more significant in the whole provision of housing for the country. So far they have been responsible for the provision of more than 500 000 houses.

In Liverpool the active housing co-operatives work within an organisation called CDS—a non-profit-making community-based Housing Association, registered with the Housing Corporation and established in 1977. It works in three areas—the rehabilitation of houses for rent, low cost co-ownership schemes and the servicing of independent housing co-operatives.

Liverpool. The Weller Street Co-operative, born in the city from 'frustration and anger', now experienced in self-management after rebuilding the community on the site of the old houses.

In Liverpool, as elsewhere, the main problem is money. The co-operatives receive 80 to 90 per cent of their money in the form of Housing Association grants. With the new Housing Act's reduction of that grant to 30 per cent, however, there will be pressure on them to raise money elsewhere—mainly in the private sector. But the co-operatives, despite their financial difficulties, can produce significant social benefits. They work from 'bottom up', generating social cohesion, commitment and identity. This seems especially clear in contrast to other major housing programmes.

The Militant group of the Liverpool Council, for example, built 5000 houses between 1983 and 1987. It was a massive investment by any standards, but was not carried out with the social awareness and sensitivity displayed by the co-operatives. The result is that already many of these two-storey houses are vandalised and unlettable, chiefly, it is said, because the tenants were housed at random without consultation. The co-operatives' approach is more rounded and considers people. It deals not just with tenure but with the whole issue of 'home', from design to environment.

The Weller Street Co-operative in Liverpool is the longest estab-lished co-operative in the city, born (in its own words) from 'frus-tration and anger'. Its members used to live in terraced streets of Dickensian two-up, two-down houses, with street names like Micawber, Copperfield and Nickleby. They were in very poor condi-tion. As one man said, all his house had to offer was a view of the Anglican cathedral from his outside toilet.

The members of the Co-operative wanted to control how and where they lived, but they also wanted to stay together as a com-munity. After five years of discussion and argument they began building on site. In 1982 the first family moved in.

There are now 61 houses in four courts, well landscaped and with sufficient space for off-street parking. Each court has a few flats for old people, and these have gardens. With two years' experience of self-management, the Weller Street tenants not only occupy them-selves with day-to-day responsibilities of management, but can also offer support to other local groups. Being their own landlords, they have power to fix rents at a reasonable level.

Rebirth of the Merchant City. Glasgow's tobacco merchants built handsome warehouses near the river Clyde. Now they have a new life as smart flats in the city centre.

In Glasgow, the local authority took a different and significant initiative. It joined forces with Housing Associations to refurbish tenements and give repair grants to owner occupiers. In the private sector, the Merchant City project in the city centre has converted commercial building to domestic use and brought people back to the city. The local authority also has schemes for homesteading—individuals or collectives can buy and improve poor quality housing with the aid of improvement grants. The two goals—of extending choice and improving stock—thus go hand in hand. People are returning to the city and, in their turn, creating new developments. And there is a further advantage. The local authority itself found that large-scale redevelopments failed; people were resentful about moving to peripheral estates. The Housing Associations, managing less than 1000 dwellings, are more popular, and always more successful.

The distinctive features of community based Housing Associations are that all members are required to live nearby and that comprehensive renewal must be carried out. Members should be on hand, committed to improving an area in which they live and work. The achievements have been outstanding—clean stone, new windows and new roofs transforming the decaying slums which were due for demolition.

A different example of current Housing Association work can be seen in rural North Wales. The Welsh Office recognises the need for social housing, especially in rural areas. Welsh Housing Associations are smaller than their English counterparts. The biggest of them have less than 2000 houses. The Welsh Housing Corporation is anxious not to become like the Northern Ireland Housing Executive, a landlord and centralised. The Welsh Housing Corporation is an enabler rather than a landlord, and wants to keep Housing Associations local. This can be a problem in rural areas as properties tend to be scattered, which means that the tenant can easily lose touch with the management. On the other hand, decentralisation is possible in rural areas, without huge resources being pumped into staffing; in the public sector, Llanelli Council, for example, has solved the problem of bringing service to the people by having a mobile housing office which can plug into the town hall computer. The high standard of service from Housing Associations is thought to stem from the fact that they are small-scale, not large-scale landlords.

By the end of the 1970s two further pieces of legislation made major changes in the housing scene. In 1977 the Housing Homeless Persons Act made it incumbent upon local authorities to find accommodation for all people who could show that they had no home. This led directly to what came to be known as the 'bed and breakfast' policy—the temporary accommodation of families on supplementary benefit.

The problem of homeless people appears to be intractable. It has now reached unprecedented figures. The total of 102 980 households reported in 1986 to be homeless rose by 11 per cent in 1987 and is thought to have doubled since then. The figures apply only to heads of households registered as homeless. The charitable action group, Shelter, estimates that there are at least 250 000 people without homes in England and Wales.

The figures for homelessness must be greater than those recognised by the Homeless Persons Act, for homelessness ought to include those in temporary accommodation as well as those in overcrowded homes. While there are thousands of people who have nowhere to live, many more are forced to live in such poor conditions that they can in effect be classified as 'homeless'.

The principal cause of homelessness must, of course, be that there is not enough accommodation available. The reasons for this are many. There has been a dramatic cut in housing expenditure. Since 1979 the amount of public money invested in housing has been cut by 40 per cent. Too few new council houses and Housing Association houses have been built for rent. Much needed repairs to the housing stock have not been carried out; the total bill for housing repairs in England is thought to be of the order of £45 billion. Above all, the decline of the private rented sector has exacerbated the problem. For many young people, buying a property is out of the question, and they are unlikely to be offered council housing as they are not considered a priority.

People become homeless for a variety of reasons. In Sutton, Shelter carried out a study of 26 year olds over a two month period. They discovered that 50 per cent did not leave their previous home deliberately. They were forced out by parental or partner violence. Others had been discharged from institutions with no home to go to.

And homelessness is not just a matter of statistics. One harrowing case reported by Shelter was that of an old age pensioner:

> Mrs S is 70 years old and living in a garage in the Isle of Wight. She pays £5 a week rent for the garage, and has to use the lavatory across the road. She has decorated the garage with flowers and tried to make it look like a house. However, she says it is a squash when the car is parked at night, and the smell from the fumes distresses her.

Once her plight had been publicised, Mrs S was rehoused. Others have been less fortunate. More homeless households than ever before are being placed in bed and breakfast hotels. Yet bed and breakfast accommodation is a dubious solution to the problem. It has debilitating side effects. The mental and physical health of both children and adults can deteriorate.

Lord Pitt, President of the British Medical Association and Chairman of Shelter, expressed his concern about the implications of bed and breakfast accommodation:

> The experience of homeless families in the eighties is causing particular health problems among the young. A recent report has shown that approximately one third of children in bed and breakfast hotel accommodation have behavioural problems. . . . Depression is endemic among the hotel homeless. Many are probably being prescribed tranquillisers. I know that in many instances doctors would prefer to prescribe new houses, not more valium. . . . I, for one, am prepared to say, on the basis of present evidence, that our current housing crisis is affecting the health of a significant number of my fellow citizens.

Not only is bed and breakfast accommodation a health risk, it is also a bad economic bargain. Recent Department of the Environment figures show that it is cheaper for local authorities to refurbish or buy homes for rent than to house homeless families in hotels. The government accepts that it costs £10 950 a year to keep a family in bed and breakfast accommodation. It would cost £5500 a year in interest payments and management costs to build a new council flat for the same family.

To rehouse everyone now living in hotels, 12 500 more decent rented homes would be needed by 1989. Government rules prevent local authorities from investing in such badly needed homes. The councils must pick up the £100 million a year hotel bill, when £56 million would provide new homes for the people now in bed and breakfast accommodation.

In Wandsworth, London, there are currently 3400 families in bed and breakfast hotels. In order to reduce this number, the council is renting flats in the private sector to house some homeless people. Brighton currently has a total of 130 families in bed and breakfast accommodation, costing the council more than £150 000 per annum. There, however, the council has leased redundant married quarters in the local barracks, bought up some properties, leased others from private landlords, and converted an old sheltered home into single units. In co-operation with the YMCA it is setting up a purpose built hostel in the town centre. Nottingham was one of the first authorities to have a purpose built hostel for the homeless. It plans to add a second hostel shortly.

If the Homeless Persons Act placed immediate responsibilities upon local authorities, the other piece of legislation was more far-reaching. Under the Housing Act of 1936, local authorities had acquired the power to sell their houses to the tenants, or indeed to anyone wishing to buy, subject to the consent of the Minister. The results were variable. By 1968, the policy of the local authorities selling council houses had become a political issue. In 1980, the Housing Act changed the procedure to what came to be known as the Right to Buy (RTB).

Tenants had previously been allowed to buy their houses if the authority was willing. Now the authority had to sell whenever the tenant wished to buy. The new Right to Buy regulations also increased discounts on the assessed value of the property and introduced tenants' rights to a mortgage.

The tenants' response to RTB was overwhelming. If the rate of sales achieved in 1980 was higher than in any previous year, in 1982 it reached a new record of over 200 000 dwellings in England and Wales. Subsequently the rate of sales declined; but by 1986 one million council and new town dwellings had been sold in Great Britain. It was the 'sale of the century'.

The popularity of RTB varies from place to place, usually reflecting the good or bad management of the estate by the local authority, and the employment situation. Inevitably there are problems. RTB purchasers are often people from working backgrounds, who have been through several housing changes. Their income drops sharply as they move into their fifties and sixties, sometimes leaving them unable to cope with maintenance. This can coincide with the property requiring major rehabilitation. Some elderly people, for instance, who welcome the chance to buy their own homes, are less happy when the bills come in for repairs. The more thoughtful have taken out insurance policies to cover repairs. The combined mortgage payments and insurance can often be less than the local authority rent.

It is too early to assess the effect of the RTB upon housing. But it must make wholesale changes unlikely ever again. With different ownerships, both public and private, in the same scheme or terrace, it would be difficult to clear it all again. Comprehensive development is therefore unlikely and, in any case, by now unpopular.

In addition to the legislation, a number of major reports and events changed the whole public attitude towards housing. In 1985 Alice Coleman published *Utopia on Trial*, the most sweeping condemnation of local authority housing ever produced. Subtitled *Vision and Reality in Planned Housing*, it was an indictment not only of the local authorities, but also of central government. It analysed, on the basis of comprehensive surveys, a number of items such as vandalism, graffiti, litter, excrement, and the number of children in care. All the results suggested that the local authorities had failed disastrously in terms of management as well as in terms of design.

Coleman's starting point was to study the dilemma in relation to the people living on the estate. Her research proved that design had a noticeable impact on behaviour. She fastened on the Department of the Environment the ultimate responsibility for what she called 'socially disadvantaging designs'. The housing types that came in for most criticism were the five or six-storey blocks with balcony access, virtually an open invitation to criminals. Her work suggested that breaking down the long balcony walkways into shorter spaces, which could be more easily supervised by tenants, would help to provide the 'defensible space' made popular by the American writer Oscar Newman. Bad housing, in short, could be attributable not only to bad design, but also to bad management.

Her report received enthusiastic support from the Audit Commission in its own report, *Managing the Crisis in Council Housing* (1986). That study is sharply critical of how local authorities have managed their housing since the war. The main theme of the study is that the housing crisis is chiefly attributable to bad design and management. Its solutions are generally managerial ones. If the two areas of activity which have handicapped mass housing since it was erected—good management and good maintenance—could be assured, there would still be hope for the housing situation.

The major movement which seems to be having a direct and positive effect upon the scene is what has come to be known as 'community architecture'. Studies of mass housing confirmed that good management and proper maintenance were essential to the happiness and health of the tenants. But, above all, tenants were commenting that they wished to have a larger share in the management of their homes. The key to the rediscovery of the great housing tradition and the creation of a satisfactory environment might lie in the involvement of communities.

Press reports have concentrated on the criticisms and comments of Prince Charles. Speaking at the 150th Anniversary celebrations of the Royal Institute of British Architects at Hampton Court in 1984, he said:

> For far too long, it seems to me, some planners and architects have consistently ignored the feelings and wishes of the mass of ordinary people in this country.... To be concerned about the way people live, about the environment they inhabit and the kind of community that is created by that environment, should surely be one of the prime requirements of a really good architect.... What I believe is important about community architecture is that it has shown 'ordinary' people that their views are worth having—that architects and planners do not necessarily have the monopoly of knowing best about taste, style and planning.

A number of pioneering projects in England have demonstrated, through community architecture, that the housing scene can be dramatically improved. The renovation of Lea View House was the first project in which local authority tenants in London were wholly involved in the rehabilitation of their homes. Before refurbishment, Lea Road was a typical problem estate, difficult to let, beset by crime and racial tension, continually vandalised. Ninety per cent of its tenants wanted to leave.

After renovation, crime and vandalism virtually disappeared. Health and spirits improved. There was a renewed sense of community. Tenant Dolly Pritchard said: 'I just want to walk around my place, I'm so chuffed with it. ... Once people fought to leave Lea View—now they're all wanting to get in. ... we are beginning to get a real good community once again.'

In contrast, the Wigan Estate, renovated just before Lea View by the same authority but without tenant involvement, soon reverted to a slum. As Prince Charles said, 'If people have played a part in creating something they treat it as their own possession and look after it.'

John Thompson, the architect for Lea View, commented on the difference between the Wigan and Lea View estates: 'It is a vivid example of how social behaviour responds to design. ... Lea View is housing for people. ... Wigan is unit housing, committee housing ... uncaring in both its execution and its management.' If design has an effect on behaviour—an obvious fact that social theorists have frequently rejected—the involvement of tenants in the management of their estates is even more important.

In Liverpool in 1982, an estate of 61 houses was opened in Toxteth, the scene of many riots. Instead of an official opening ceremony, there was a street party lasting till four o'clock in the morning. The manager of the construction company involved in the project said it was the first time he had known the names of all his clients, including the children. The *Architects Journal* reported:

Something incredible has happened in Liverpool—arguably the most important step forward in British housing for decades. Without anyone else in the country really noticing it, an era spanning fifty years of paternalistic public housing provision has quietly come to an end. In its place a new way of building publicly funded housing has taken over in which the users are firmly in the driving seat.

The involvement of the people in the design and management of their housing is clearly an important development. A different approach has been adopted by the North of Ireland Housing Executive. Housing in Northern Ireland may look much the same as that on the mainland, but its organisation and management is in fact radically different. Its administration was drastically changed in a way which sets it apart from other parts of Great Britain. With considerable difficulty the various agencies and authorities responsible for public housing in Ireland were dissolved in 1971 and one major housing organisation formed, the Northern Ireland Housing Executive.

Part of the reason for this was the division of the communities into Catholic and Protestant areas, sometimes separated by walls or barriers erected between sections or even sectors. The policy of the Housing Executive was not, however, to emphasise the division, but to treat all parts of their society in the same way. There is no distinction between housing types or space provisions for the different communities.

More money is available than in the rest of the British Isles; the result has been a higher standard of houses and landscapes. The Housing Executive is responsible for some 200 000 dwellings. The least attractive—and generally condemned—are the flats in Belfast known as the Divis flats, eventually fit only for demolition.

The present housing policy combines several approaches, most of which are concerned with preservation rather than innovation, but all of which have lessons relevant to the rest of the country.

At a fairly low density, the chief components of rehabilitation are 'infill' (filling spaces in existing developments), 'facelifts' (where houses worth preserving are refurbished), and 'enveloping' (where the exterior is brought up to a reasonable standard and the interior is left to the owner or tenant). The Executive has followed the policy of using similar house types but varying the external treatments. Different architects worked to certain standardised house plans and produced different solutions, mostly traditional, but varied in relation to the porches, gardens and their paved areas.

Some of the most attractive are where colour has been used

116

Poleglass, the biggest estate planned, built and managed by the North of Ireland Housing Executive. Warm and homely with a diversity of colours, details, materials and planting.

boldly on exteriors, and when paintings (even political statements) have enlivened the gables of blocks. Some of the most successful layouts can be seen at Poleglass and in smaller, more intimate schemes, such as those at Downpatrick.

What remains unsolved, except in rare cases, are two continuing dilemmas. First, the fact that this country has never been able to provide quality housing that the ordinary man and woman can afford without public subsidy. The present government has not shown how this can happen—how an affordable rent is possible without subsidy.

Sir Ernest Simon wrote in *Half A Century of Municipal Reform* (1935):

> One vital point that must be remembered is that we cannot get the families of the lower paid workers out of the slums unless we build new houses for them at rent within their means. If we are able to house the present slum population in new houses of the Tudor Walters type, we must face the fact that very substantial subsidies will be required.

117

Simon's comment on the perennial failure of government to deal with the housing of the poor is as valid today as when he noted that fact in 1935. State intervention can improve the condition of houses, but by doing so it can also force up costs and, therefore, rents.

The second problem is that of rented housing, its scarcity and cost. The government may hope that all housing will, in due course, be owner-occupied. Evidence suggests that this will never be fully achieved.

Above all, there remains the problem of numbers. How are the large numbers of people needing accommodation to be housed? Is it managerially practicable to supply enough housing through small organisations? Can Housing Associations cope with the numbers without becoming large and impersonal, indistinguishable from local authorities? Is it possible to house the homeless without the help of local authorities?

The great tradition—of humane housing on small sites with user involvement—suggests that the answer cannot lie in mass schemes, high or low. What is needed is a variety of solutions and experiments. In short, a change from a monolithic to a pluralistic system. That would, after all, reflect the pluralistic character of the society for which housing is needed.

What, at the very least, is clear is that the era of the grandiose architectural concept is at an end. Housing will never be the vehicle for great architecture again.

CHAPTER SIX

WHOSE GREEN AND PLEASANT LAND?

The story of housing, as told in this book, started with the influx of people moving from the country into the towns during the Industrial Revolution. Now, in the 1980s, after several more social and economic revolutions, the traffic is the other way round. If the first crisis was the overcrowding of the towns, the new crisis is the danger to the countryside—and to the life of the country—from the new rural enthusiasts who have never experienced rural living.

Their aspiration is the same as that of the planners and theorists of the nineteenth century—the delectable country cottage. For what the ordinary man and woman wanted, and still want, was not, on the whole, grand monuments; it was represented, rather, by the garden cities and by most of the housing erected since 1919. That housing continued, even in the hectic days of high-rise housing, in every town and every part of the country; and still does.

Very few people want an impossible fantasy or dream. Their desires are usually a combination of what they would like to have, and what they know or imagine is available. And the remarkable thing is that such a combination is frequently to be found—after much searching—on the ground. It is some kind of cottage. Or some kind of bungalow.

It was written into the Tudor Walters Report, which, as we have seen, formed the practical basis of the famous Addison Act of 1919. Of the type of accommodation required by the working classes, the Report discussed several alternative designs and had no doubt that the most suitable and popular was 'the self-contained cottage'.

The self-contained cottage had 'continued to be the customary means of housing in Britain despite the rapid development of large towns and cities'. The 'freedom from tenement dwellings' characteristic of the British Isles was regarded, the Report said, with envy by 'those countries and cities which had the misfortune to adopt the tenement system'.

Since Raymond Unwin was a member of the Tudor Walters

Committee, it was not surprising that the self-contained cottage, of which he was a superb exponent, was its main recommendation for most of the country.

Critics might deplore the disappearance of acres of grass under houses, preferably less than 12 to the acre. They might also lament the lining of all the roads spreading out from the towns and cities in what was castigated as 'ribbon development'. But the fact was that between the wars, the housing needs of the big industrial cities were met largely by building where there was the most available land—namely in the country. The town spilled over into the countryside.

During the 20 years between the two wars, four million houses were built in England—enough to accommodate almost a third of her inhabitants. Of these a significant number, if not always cottages, were suburban dwellings—often bungalows.

The suburb has a respectable history and a reputation that, having gone down between the two world wars, is now as high as it was in late Victorian times.

The first garden suburb was that of Bedford Park in Chiswick, started in 1875. It was leafy and informal, following the lines of existing boundaries and the architectural styles of Norman Shaw and (later) Charles Voysey. It was convenient for the station—a fact that had a crucial bearing on the development of all suburbs.

Suburban trains made possible the spread of the towns for people of moderate means. Within a few years the major cities had elaborate networks of suburban lines. They were followed, by the end of the century, by the trams and then—in the twentieth century—by buses everywhere and by the Underground in London. For everyone, especially the less affluent, the spread of the suburbs was given a helping hand by the Cheap Trains Act of 1883.

The growth of the suburbs was thus an inevitable consequence of urban development. It initiated the now commonplace, then revolutionary, separation of work and leisure. In a visible way the suburbs reflected the changing economic structure of society. They provided the basis for Betjeman's love affair with what he called *Metroland*.

In 1929, almost any land in Britain was potential building land. If development on a certain plot of land was forbidden for any reason, the owner could be compensated for the loss of possible profit.

The houses were of the type now taken so much for granted that they are almost invisible—neo-Tudor and then neo-Georgian in

The evolution of the suburb, mock Tudor in Chiswick.
The ideal English middle-class house, a total success and
copied everywhere.

style, bungalows and the ubiquitous semi-detached house in type. By
the end of the 1930s, an area stretching 15 miles from the centre of
London was covered in houses built at 12 or 14 to the acre.

Many families were inspired by the idea of moving from the town
to the country. The healthier and more social environment, the
escape from the dirt, noise, congestion and often the isolation of the
city were all attractive propositions. It was thought there would be
more of 'a real home' in a rural setting.

Ebenezer Howard, after all, had evolved these same ideas some
years earlier at the turn of the century: 'Town and Country must be
married and out of this joyous union will spring a new hope, a new
life, and a new civilisation.' Improved transport facilities gave this
ideal the possibility of implementation.

Not everybody was so idealistic or impressed by the urban
sprawl. The *Builder*, for example, expressed alarm at the building
boom of the 1930s. Over 3.9 million homes had been built by the end
of this period, mostly in suburbia:

121

> East, west, north and south our cities and towns are extending them-
> selves into the country. ... Houses spring up everywhere, as though
> capital were abundant, as though one-half of the world were on the look-
> out for investments and the other half continually in search of desirable
> country residences. ... We are disposed to ask, in these days when we
> contemplate the number of houses in course of erection for the rich,
> where the poor are to be housed. One would think there was no increase
> of population below the classes which rejoice in five hundred a year.

Ribbon development was particularly criticised. This consisted of detached or semi-detached houses in facing rows of indefinite length, on either side of an existing or newly constructed road.

Tenants of such developments who had a pleasant rural view from their back windows seemed not to mind that the front looked onto a main road. The view of those on the road was, however, less pleasing, as their glimpse of the country was blotted out by houses. The houses themselves spoiled the harmony of the landscape, and service to the houses was extremely wasteful.

Not only did they usually ruin the appearance of the country-side, but the appearance of the homes themselves was unfortunate. They were generally over-elaborate, with many fussy embellish-ments, the whole forming a kind of pastoral pastiche. The aesthetic of the suburbs might be the bane of intellectuals; the occupants them-selves thought them artistic.

The majority of the houses were semi-detached, with three bedrooms, two living rooms, a bathroom, kitchen and garage, or a space for a garage in a small garden. Random ornament tended to ruin any architectural balance. But it produced variety.

The 'desecration' of the countryside, shortly to be lamented by the Prime Minister, Stanley Baldwin, was proceeding rapidly. In spite of some efforts to preserve a green belt around the major cities such as London, most of the periphery of the big industrial towns became built up as they still are today. The Town Planning Act of 1925 required the local authorities of towns of more than 20 000 inha-bitants to prepare plans for future development and pay particular attention to roads. Ring roads and green belts were designated—to little immediate effect.

But what of living in the suburbs? Here too opinion was divided. The aptly named *Ideal Home* urged prospective buyers to consider their house choice carefully, and recommended rural building:

> Don't rush into your acquisition of a new home. Look around and see
> what will be the best proposition for yourself and your family. ... The

latest ideas in domestic architecture and town planning can be seen by a tour of the estates which are being developed throughout the country. ('Why live in town?'—June 1929)

It was not a new problem. The question of whether to live in town or country was already an absorbing one. It had been argued as early as 1844 in *An Encyclopaedia of Domestic Economy*. There, it was suggested that the town was advantageous for theatres, concerts, balls, parties, libraries, museums and art galleries. Both cultural facilities and conveniences were adduced in its favour, as well as fashion. The benefits of the country, on the other hand, were fresh air, a wholesome environment and the joys of a garden, together with the benefits of trees and vegetation. Of potential speculative interest, the fact was that, since land was cheaper (another advantage it had over the town), an extra field might be attached to the house, which could then, of course, be built upon.

Mrs J E Panton, the author of *From Kitchen to Garret*, supported the suburbs particularly as a home for young people. In *Hints for the Young* (1888) she wrote:

To young people ... I would strongly recommend a house some little way out of London. Rents are less, smuts and blacks are conspicuous by their absence; a small garden, or even a tiny conservatory are not an impossibility; and if 'Edwin' has to pay for his season ticket, that is nothing in comparison with his being able to sleep in fresh air, or to have a game of tennis in summer ... without expense.

The suburbs which Mrs Panton recommended were, in the south, the higher parts of Sydenham, Lordship Lane, Forest Hill, Elmers End, Penge, Dulwich and Bromley, and 'to those who do not mind the north side', Finchley, Bush Hill Park and Enfield.

On the whole, contemporary opinion approved the suburbs on account of fresh air, roomier houses for families, the possession of a garden and facilities for recreation.

There were, however, serious reservations. The quality of the spec-built houses in the countryside was called into question by an article in the *Architects' Journal* in 1923. The author, Crossley Davies, praised the speculators both for answering an urgent demand and for building in the countryside, but went on to condemn the houses themselves:

We found the stairs deep and winding, perilous for children and tiring for adults. The main criticism of the bedroom floor is that the bathroom was ridiculously small. In one case the door could not be opened to the full

123

extent because the lavatory basin stopped it. Electric light was laid on, but there were no power plugs. ... This sort of thing will not do.

The time taken up by commuting was another disadvantage of the suburbs, as indeed it still is. There were many radio discussions on the pros and cons of suburbia, in which this was a major argument. In one of these, reported in the *Listener*, 'Witness A' says:

The worst of suburban life is that it wastes the one thing man cannot replace—life itself. To add hours of travel every week to a man's ordinary working day is just foolishly taking away all the advantages given by lessening hours in industry.

Another disquiet voiced in this discussion was that the suburb had no community. Amenities were not built until much later, so that at first the developments contained only houses. Any entertainment had to be sought in a now-distant town centre:

A suburb usually has no centre of its communal life. ... Human life refuses to wait; and if a generation grows up before libraries, churches and public baths are provided, a generation is created which has learnt to do without them. (*Listener*—February 1935)

Other observers became as worried by overcrowding in the country as by that already present in the town. As Yorke and Gibberd in *The Modern Flat* pointed out in 1937:

People try to escape outwards into the country, only to lose what they are seeking, because so many must seek the same open space in the same place that the countryside disappears under houses, roads and garden plots.

This too was not a new anxiety. Queen Elizabeth I was concerned with congestion when she issued a proclamation in 1580:

Charging and straightly commanding all manner of Persons of what Qualitie soever they be, to desist and forbear from any new buildings of any House or Tenement within three miles from any gate of the sayde City of London.

She was not, presumably, attempting to stop population growth: she was attempting to stop the growth of London, sprawling in an unhealthy way into the country. London, however, despite the proclamation, continued to sprawl, with the result that Elizabeth had dreaded—the spread of the plague.

Even in this less dangerous century their exponents came to see that, while they solved some of the dilemmas, in many other ways the suburbs did not work. They failed to solve London's housing problem, mainly because their economic status declined, as land values and by-laws governing building increased. The suburbs clogged and dirtied the environs of the towns, and put the country even further out of reach of city dwellers, especially children. Time, money and energy were expended on commuting, and agricultural land was eroded by houses. As Yorke and Gibberd pointed out: 'The problem of housing cannot be solved by the provision of millions of little cottages scattered over the face of the country, whether in the garden city manner, or as speculatively built stragglers.'

But however much Yorke and Gibberd might deride 'the little cottage', the fact was that the cottage was the paradigm for English housing, whether grouped together on the ground or piled up in blocks.

What Unwin achieved in the garden cities was not fundamentally different from what the local authorities tried to achieve in council estates. For both of them the English village was the animated symbol. If the cottage was the ideal dwelling for working people, the village was the ideal community for working people—as well as for all the eccentrics and oddities that make up rural society.

While the towns were marching outwards through the suburbs, what was happening to the village at the far end of the march?

In the inter-war period, council houses were usually built separately, at a short distance from the existing village, rarely if ever interspersed with older houses. Generally, they were placed in a field purchased by the authority and developed with standard houses.

The houses were both detached and semi-detached. The most economical and easily repeated of house types, the semi-detached, saved the cost of a wall, helped the heating of the house, and allowed access to the gardens from the road, without the tunnel walkways necessary in a terrace.

Some of these developments were very attractive—usually where a local landowner insisted on good traditional materials. Some, on the other hand, were outrageously out of character, like rows of inappropriate standard houses outside a homely and colourful village. A letter to the Editor of *Country Life* in 1924 bemoaned the loss of tradition and clash of styles which the new building occasioned:

> Sir, the village is small and old and any new building immediately attracts our attention and criticism. For several weeks they have been erecting two small cottages at the end of our chief street. ... They are actually using slates. ... Now, the chance traveller will walk down the row of

white-walled, thatch-crowned cottages and will just be growing interested in their old world atmosphere when he will suddenly be confronted by the uninspired grey of the new slates. Surely there is enough
slate-grey drabness in towns and cities.

Stanley Baldwin also objected to this tampering with tradition.
Speaking in Winchester, he declared:

It is no exaggeration to say that in fifty years, at the rate so-called
improvements are being made, the destruction of all the beauty and
charm with which our ancestors enhanced their towns and villages will
be complete.

If standards of council housing between the wars and after 1924 were
poor—at their best ignored, at their worst offensive—it was the
years after the Second World War that saw a more drastic change in
the character of the villages. They were both revived and renewed.

What changed their life and their appearance were two developments: firstly, the availability of money for mortgages, so that city
dwellers could have second homes or invest in cottages for their
retirement. Of the 80 houses in Cadgwith in Cornwall, for example,
10 are second and 20 are holiday homes. Secondly, there was the
unprecedented growth in communications of all kinds: telephone
links between home and work, transport to take children to schools
and an increase in the number of cars owned by commuters.

The villages which had suffered neglect before the war suddenly
had a new influx of people and money, as the country became the
most desirable place to live. The changes were both liked and
disliked. There might be benefits, especially financial ones, but the
villages would never be the same again.

The main changes were these. The sale of small houses, which
had followed Lloyd George's famous 'People's Budget' of 1909, continued after both the First and Second World Wars. Estate owners,
who had for generations lodged their workers in tied cottages, which
represented a large part of the workers' mediocre earnings, now
found it more advantageous—for reasons of revenue and taxation—
to sell their cottages.

The estate workers were moved into council houses, where they
still are; the old cottages were bought by commuters or second-home
owners. Some locals bought their cottages and then (much to the
annoyance of the original owners) sold them soon after for a handsome profit. It was probably the only capital sum they were ever
likely to make.

That probably did not matter so much in the case of isolated cottages on large estates, or those at some distance from the village. Where it did affect the economic and social life of the village was where the old houses in the village were sold and the new owners did not live in the village but came to it only occasionally, for holidays or weekends.

The effect upon the local shop, the pub and the post office could be catastrophic. The village shop might not be such an economic proposition when a large number of the house owners are commuters who buy their goods at the supermarket on the way home from work. The elderly and the second-homers cannot keep a shop going between them.

Some villages survived, as their residents recognised, because of the in-comers. The houses were improved, more money was spent and standards, correspondingly, were raised. Others were less lucky. What was clear was that the village was fundamentally altered. The old kinship patterns were disrupted and the community fell apart.

Planning law provides little or no opportunity for a site to be developed in accordance with local needs. Parish councils complain that they frequently lack control over what happens in their village. Statements about 'local needs' are discouraged, sometimes by the Department of the Environment.

On the other hand, attempts to contribute to the local good are occasionally countermanded by the residents themselves. One attractive village, for example, was desperately in need of children for its school. The director of housing, intending to raise the number of schoolchildren, lodged two divorcees and their seven children in the village—only to find that this did not go down at all well with the residents!

That villages, as a whole, will never be the same again may simply be because their social and economic basis has been fundamentally altered.

In every part of the country, but notoriously in the areas where second homes for city dwellers are popular, there are complaints that locals can no longer afford the cottage that their ancestors grew up in. That may be their own fault—if they sell the cottages for a handsome sum, move into a council house and then complain about the cost of the old house!

It does mean, however—to use the term becoming ubiquitous in such studies—that the young cannot find 'affordable' rural housing.

The shortage of such housing has different causes in different parts of the country, but the effect is the same—the old may stay where they are but the young are forced to look elsewhere.

In the village of Minstead in Hampshire, for example, young people, despite longstanding local ties, are forced by house prices to move to Totton or Southampton to live. Neither is there any property for them to rent. As one resident complained:

> I have lived in Minstead all my life and so have four previous generations of my family. My son is hoping to get married shortly to a local girl and cannot afford to buy here and there is nothing for them to rent. They have come to realise that they will have to move to Totton to get a council property.

A similar problem exists in the village of Grantchester near Cambridge, immortalised by Rupert Brooke. Grantchester is at the heart of an affluent and rapidly expanding area where the price of land has dramatically increased. Some of the local youth are reaching the age when they want their own homes; their family friends and connections are in Grantchester. The cheapest property in the village is council housing. But that is mostly sold off; and the price of the houses is already far beyond the reach of local first-time buyers.

It will not be surprising if, in a few years' time, there is no rented and no owner-occupied housing that any young person can afford. The elderly will be separated from their young families (who will have to move away) and will become increasingly isolated; they will have to lean more heavily on the Social Services, which would not be so necessary if the family was within reach. A village once renowned for farming and with a mix of the social classes will soon only be accessible to the affluent and professional.

The Chairman of West Somerset Rural Housing Association, in a recent report, highlights the scale of the dilemma and the great number of young people affected:

> A development of nine starter homes in this Exmoor village is planned. ... Since the development was announced ... a constant stream of young couples has been begging to be considered for a tenancy. They all live and work locally and can't be considered for a council house because they don't have children. ... How can they afford to buy a house in this village, in the middle of one of the country's most renowned beauty spots? We have at least twice as many applicants as we plan to have houses—and that does not include those already registered on the Council's waiting list.

The absence of the young affects all the services—shops, pubs and community centres. The young are, of course, also those on low or average incomes. The village grows smarter; the native population smaller.

Only four of the Wootton Courtenay village cricket team actually live in the village; the others travel each weekend to play from distances up to 20 miles away. This is not due to any local prejudice against cricket, but because there are hardly enough residents young enough to play. Young people have vacated Wootton Courtenay mainly because of the house prices. Their places are being taken by retired people from other parts of the country, or by second and holiday home buyers.

All of this has a cumulative effect. A young couple who might take the risk of a high mortgage, are now unwilling to move to a village where there are few young people or children and where most of the houses are empty for most of the year. But Wootton Courtenay is a fairly prosperous village. Here, as in many such villages throughout England, there are no homeless people, no substandard housing, no long waits for council houses. There are also—or soon will be—no shops, no buses, no schools, no cricket teams.

The lack of young people is not limited to depressed areas; it afflicts the affluent regions too. But here nonetheless, there is a disparity between local house prices and local earnings. As village earnings tend to be modest, village houses can only be afforded by outsiders with more lucrative city jobs. This is especially true of young people. Apart from the young being naturally less well paid than their elders, employment in rural districts tends to be in low-wage industries—farming, tourism and leisure. Even those in professional posts find their salaries do not match house prices.

Government encouragement to high-tech industries to move to rural areas may not help either. Such industries are often placed in attractive villages, because they draw keen young executives, offering them an alternative lifestyle to the city. They also force up house prices. The discrepancy in salaries makes a huge social divide. Banks are notorious for making public statements about their support for the small trader and equally notorious for not helping him.

Unemployment is also common in rural areas, and makes housing still more unobtainable. In Clive in Shropshire, for example, agriculture and sandstone quarrying are the main sources of employment. Unfortunately quarrying is in decline, and dairy farming has been affected by quotas. As far as housing is concerned the rented sector has almost disappeared. For those who could not afford to buy, renting used to be the obvious short-term resource. Now the shortage of houses for rent in such rural areas is serious.

The problem, as always, seems to be primarily one of shortage. Demand for houses to buy in the country rises as the supply falls. Similarly the demand for rented accommodation rises at a time when there has never been less of it.

The Rural Department of Hampshire Council, in conjunction with parish councils, carried out surveys of housing needs in a number of villages. In the village of Beaulieu in the New Forest, the survey discovered 19 households which needed local housing to rent. Many of these households were newly married or engaged couples who would be given no priority on a district council's waiting list. To have priority you need to be unwell or to have children. In that district the ratio of applicants in priority need to vacancies available is already four to one. These are only the priority cases; the overall figure must be higher.

A National Trust land agent made the following statement:

> The National Trust owns over 60 houses and cottages on the Mottisfont estate in Hampshire. . . . The Trust's lettings policy is to ensure that it has housing available for the employees necessary for the management of the estate. . . . Once these requirements have been met, any vacancy is offered to people on our waiting list, with priority being given to people with family or local connections with the village. In practice the turnover of tenancies is very small and the waiting list relatively long, so that it is probably true that most people on the list will never be housed by us. This must also have the effect of discouraging applications.

There is also a shortage of purpose built housing for the elderly. They may wish to move to more appropriate housing, which is only available in a town. They often remain in large council houses which are too large for them to manage and might otherwise be available for young families.

On the positive side of the rural question, some very good work has been or is being done by Housing Associations. The drawback is that the Associations, like private developers, may be unable to build housing that the less affluent can afford. New housing built for sale is primarily the detached expensive kind or the retirement bungalow—both unsuitable for the young.

A disadvantage of the Associations is that they tend to be based in towns; the needs of the cities have their immediate attention and absorb most of their resources. But there are some constructive projects in the offing. A number of new Housing Associations have been set up to build houses for rent in small villages. They now exist in eight counties. The schemes have revealed the extent of the need.

The Development Commission (the government agency for the development of rural areas in England) though not a housing authority, has nevertheless a limited budget from which to subsidise housing schemes. The Housing Corporation, funded by central government, also contributes to rural Housing Association projects, but its funding is unevenly spread over a restricted number of villages, most of the time quite out of proportion to need. And 87 per cent of the Housing Corporation's funds has to be allocated to urban stress areas.

A possible solution, increasingly discussed, is the system of shared ownership—where the owner pays 50 per cent of the equity, and pays a subsidised rent on the remainder. That system accepts values dictated by the market, but at the same time allows people on modest incomes to become part-owners. If more funding were available for rented or shared ownership, sites of a half to two-thirds of an acre in many villages could be put to constructive use.

There are many disadvantages to shared ownership. The DoE sets unrealistic values on the properties concerned, which makes it impossible to design houses that keep within the limits. Another difficulty is that the low rent subsidy depends on the part-owner being offered full ownership when he wants it. Ultimately this means that the houses become part of the private rented sector. They are no longer economical, and cannot be reserved for local people.

Another possible answer is to rely on other (non Housing Corporation) subsidies. Such bodies are not numerous. In 1982–84 two such agencies jointly funded a project of shared ownership in 16 villages. It was partially successful. About 100 households were helped. The figure aimed at had been considerably higher.

A factor that must soon have a bearing on the situation is the government's decision to redesignate the use of agricultural land from farming (which is too productive) to open space, forestry or housing. Farmers are rarely unwilling to make money out of anything at hand, and if large areas of farmland can be redesignated for housing, fortunes will be made. Both farmers and development companies, with their eyes on the main chance, are waiting to see what

Terrington on the first ridge of the Howardian Hills above the plain of York—everything the classic village should have but might be swamped in the 'Yorkshire Cotswolds'.

can be done. Many hundreds of acres of land are being watched, especially in regions where the demand is known. East Anglia and parts of North Yorkshire (the Yorkshire Cotswolds) may be transformed as a result.

Positive action has been taken in many areas. In Dent in Cumbria, a survey of housing needs was undertaken in 1983 by the parish council, in conjunction with Cumbria Council for Voluntary Action. The survey revealed a need for low cost housing, both bought and rented, for the young, and rented housing for the elderly. The parish council found a suitable site and approached the owner. The latter lived in London, but was willing to sell the site in order to help local people—it was a positive example of landowner, government and voluntary organisations working together.

In 1985, South Lakeland District Council funded four rented homes for retired people. In this case the Parish Council, the Council for Voluntary Action, the Yorkshire Dales National Park, the Housing Corporation, the Council, the Development Commission, the landowner and the Two Castles Housing Association all contributed to the success of the venture.

132

Even in Minstead in Hampshire, one of the worst-hit villages, plans to redress imbalance are afoot. A group of local people, assisted by the New Forest District Council, formed the New Forest Villages Housing Association. Within weeks it had planned and gained permission for a development containing five first-time homes and three homes for the elderly—all funded by the Housing Corporation. Owing to funding delays, the earliest building could start was the summer of 1988.

The report, *Village Homes for Village People*, published by the NAC Rural Trust in 1987, debates many rural housing issues. It also provides brief descriptions of villages where it is known there is a need, and where attempts have been made to answer it.

The villages it cites include Timberscombe in Somerset, where a new Rural Housing Association has been formed, and Corringham in Lincolnshire, where the Housing Corporation is to develop four bungalows for the elderly and two family houses for rent. In West Burton, in North Yorkshire, the village Housing Association, *Sanctuary*, purchased a site with great difficulty assisted by the NAC Rural Trust. They planned to build four family houses and three low price bungalows for the elderly. Only the amount required to buy that site was initially released by the Housing Corporation. Funds to allow building to begin could not be awarded until 1988 at the earliest.

With a few basic alterations in policy, the rural scene in housing could be very different. If the government were to allocate more funds to the Housing Corporation specifically for village schemes, and district councils were to fund small Housing Association developments of up to six houses per village, the state of rural housing would be vastly improved.

Other vital improvements would be for the Development Commission to encourage Housing Associations to give village schemes priority, and support locally based studies and surveys of village housing needs, in addition to financing housing projects through the 'topping up' fund.

Housing Associations could better their work in the country if they accepted that village schemes work best by listening to and involving the community. The rural communities' councils might similarly ensure that Associations work closely with rural inhabitants.

County councils can make a significant contribution by backing developments in small communities where occupancy is restricted to locals, as well as studying ways in which surplus land and property can be sold at historic cost rather than at current value to locally based Housing Associations.

District councils could rejuvenate the housing scene by accepting that Housing Associations, particularly those that are locally based, can make as meaningful a contribution to the problem as district councils, and work alongside them. They could also help by reporting village housing needs and dilemmas to the Department of the Environment, and by giving grant aid to village Housing Association projects to counterbalance the land costs.

Still the situation remains volatile and potentially disastrous. David Carrow, a retired company director who lives in the hectically growing region of 'silicon valley' south of Reading, expressed the problem with some force. Proposals for expansion were, he said 'getting on for 50 000 people and the population at the moment is something around 80 000 ... the district has already doubled in the last 20 years ... unless we stop at some point this will be the black country of the twenty-first century.' The reasons were simple and obvious:

> One of the problems of our district is that we have become a commuter area for all the surrounding districts. ... All the way round here there's been in-filling and accretions on the outside. Hook has more than doubled, Yateley has multiplied by four times. Yateley was a tiny little village. ... The village of Hartley Wintney has more than doubled in the last 20 years.

He looks forward to the day 'when the housing bubble bursts'. It is unlikely to burst without government intervention and financial policies that halt or at least delay the dramatic rise in house prices, which are ultimately affected by the supply or shortage of land. Planning policies, including the designation of green belts to prevent the spread of towns that occurred so relentlessly between the wars, have made land with planning permission for the erection of houses effectively a gold mine. In areas such as that south of Reading, there seems no end to the possibility of housing spreading indefinitely other than positive planning policies, popular with residents who deplore the prospect of endless housing and unpopular with landowners who see a fortune looming up ahead of them. And there are other problems.

The Reverend Neil Davies, who has recently moved to Lower Earley, a vast spreading settlement of about 6000 houses promising to get bigger, spoke of some of the problems encountered by the new

The city advances into the countryside. Lower Earley, Berkshire, the largest spec-built housing scheme. No end to the demand, acres of land still to be gobbled up.

residents—not knowing their neighbours, isolation and stress, defaults on mortgage payments, and the transitory nature of their society; people have to go where the work is and they move in only a few years: 'The shopping centre started first and the housing grew around it ... the actual community centre, the pub, the library, the church, that came much later....'

The fact is that the houses erected by the speculative builders have been a success. Changing ever so slightly from site to site and responding to the demands of a market well understood by the developers, the spec-builders' housing has become mass housing, better than public housing because it is planned in smaller groups, and meeting a need because its designers are not architects with a vision but pragmatists with a clear eye on potential purchasers. So even if its occupiers complain about traffic congestion in getting into and out of their new arcadias, they seem contented with their houses. The Reverend Neil Davies sees a much more fundamental need and one which has always been central in the history of housing. 'It's a very nebulous concept', but he wanted to see 'a community spirit and help to forge a community'. That is the nub of the problem. Neither legislation nor speculative development can do that. People will have to work it out for themselves.

CHAPTER SEVEN

THE PEOPLE IN CHARGE?

A group of local government officials reported to NALGO in 1973: 'There will never be a time at which housing problems will be solved: housing is simply not capable of that kind of simplistic treatment.' They were right. But the impossibility of achieving perfection does not remove the obligation of behaving well. Attempts to improve conditions have been continuous and sometimes dramatic. And what they have revealed is the scale and complexity of the problems. It seems appropriate at the end of this book to bring the problems together by concentrating on one case study.

The example is Easterhouse—a huge estate on the periphery of Glasgow with nearly 13 000 houses and more than 40 000 people. Easterhouse is considered by many commentators to be possibly the most unsuccessful housing project ever completed in this country. It has been accused of being simply a device for storing up thousands of people without any of the social facilities which make life tolerable and fit for human activity.

But Easterhouse has to be seen against the background of the city of Glasgow. The city of Glasgow is the largest municipal landlord in the country, with some 165 000 dwellings. This represents 57 per cent of the city's housing stock. Although that majority tenure has declined since the Right to Buy (RTB) legislation, there are nevertheless large parts of the city which have single tenure, particularly the peripheral estates, such as Easterhouse, built in the 1950s and the 1960s. There are four such major peripheral estates, each of which has a massive 10 000 dwellings, nearly all in three to four-storey walk-up blocks which are usually described as tenements.

The city seems to be on its way to sorting out many of its housing problems, particularly those in the 'inner city'. In that inner city the local authority has joined forces with Housing Associations to rehabilitate tenements and give repair grants to owner-occupiers. The transformation of the city is already remarkable. With the Merchant City project, Victorian commercial buildings have been converted to domestic use, and this has been hugely successful in bringing people back into the city. There has also been great emphasis on community based Housing Associations managing less than 1000 dwellings each.

It is the peripheral estates which now constitute the major problem. Monotonous in form and appearance, generally single tenure, with poor amenities and high unemployment, they reveal a housing stock in poor condition which was built in a hurry and now needs repairs all at once. Most of them were built to very low standards, with inadequate heating and certainly with inadequate insulation. Most of them are two to three-bedroom walk-up family apartments.

Easterhouse has a complex of buildings that passes for a town centre. For a population of more than 40 000 people, there is one supermarket, no public house, no cinema and one café. There is one bookmaker and one bank. The bookie has the highest turnover in Europe, and the bank is said to charge £20 to clear a cheque. There is a travel agent who is very busy: perhaps everyone is fleeing. The people of Easterhouse are well accustomed to queueing—they queue for everything.

Glasgow, like other cities, has been affected by the 'Right to Buy'. Out of its 165 000 houses more than 6000 have been bought through RTB, though very few on the Easterhouse estate. Of those who have, the majority had an Easterhouse connection—they were not newcomers coming in from outside.

It is thought by officials that if the housing department can get the product right, people will come back to Easterhouse. In any event there is now a choice opening up for the first time—council tenure, homesteading, owner-occupation, soon to be joined by new semis and bungalows for sale. It is in fact becoming a mixed infrastructure. The Cruden rehabilitation development for sale in South Rogerfield is the fastest selling development in the country. Twenty-four of the houses in this development have been kept for rent in their rehabilitated state, and it is difficult to tell which they are. Many of the South Rogerfield houses have been bought by people in their twenties. The work has been so successful that the developer wishes to build on vacant land behind—houses, not flats, and including sheltered housing managed by the West of Scotland Housing Association.

Easterhouse has 12 700 houses. Forty-four per cent of the tenants are in receipt of full housing benefit and pay nothing for their houses. Seventy-four per cent of tenants receive some benefit.

Unemployment is about 35 per cent, male unemployment is over 60 per cent, youth unemployment is over 70 per cent.

There are now five community renewal projects where tenants, architects and the housing department have got together to work out what needs to be done. Tenants, when consulted in this way, tend to look at the wider implications of what they want.

In making our TV programme we decided to look in some detail at the Calvay Street Co-operative. The Calvay Street Co-operative was founded by Frances McColl. In her view, it is not just the houses that need attention; the most important thing for the future is bringing work and business back to the area. Houses are the beginning, not the end of the story. But in Frances McColl's view, tenants need knowledge and information to transform their lives, and they need to learn how to get these. The Co-op has been in operation for some 18 months, though that was preceded for five years by a steering group. The Co-op was able to acquire the houses from the local authority; it then received a 100 per cent grant from the Housing Corporation. There were, of course, barriers between bodies and organisations before the Co-op got the money. The Housing Department of the city council was very supportive; the council itself less so. The situation is now much better. The improved flats cost about £7 a month more than an unimproved one.

Before they started rebuilding, the protagonists sat for many months discussing the problems and the priorities. Frances McColl, the architect and the housing manager talked to me about some of the factors that had played a part in the transformation of this formerly exceedingly unattractive estate. Why was the work done? 'The area', said Frances, 'was in a state of decay, and the tenants were fed up with living in it and getting what they considered a very poor service. They found the Co-operative had a better quality of house and a better quality of service from the landlord.'

But who are the Co-operative? Frances McColl was quite clear: 'The tenants are the same tenants who were there before. The tenants don't own anything, the Co-operative is run by the tenants, but the Co-operative is owned actually by itself. ... First of all,' she pointed out, 'we've improved the homes that the council didn't have the money to do, and I think that's the first step. Secondly we can give ourselves a better repair service. It is a co-operative venture on behalf of the tenants, but it is a local initiative from the Glasgow District Council and the tenants together, and now a partnership

The Calvay Street project at Easterhouse, Glasgow.
Desolate standard housing transformed by local initiative
and architectural imagination.

The photographs on these pages show the Easterhouse project before, during and after the transformation. Also shown are an enthusiastic supporter of the project and its architect (in conversation with the author).

between the Co-op, the Council and the Scottish Office, so it's quite a unique package.'

I asked Frances McColl what was the difference between the Co-operative and the Council when the tenants of the Co-op were after all the same people who were tenants of the Council.

'Well,' she replied, 'the difference is that the tenants have taken on the responsibility of allocating the houses, generally keeping the property up to standard, and also rebuilding the community. When you build up credibility as a co-op you can then tap into resources for other things in your area.'

'It's early days yet,' she said, 'but we've supplied some of the facilities. I think what we are looking to is that these facilities have to be provided by ourselves, and I think the climate for the tenants of public sector stock is changing because they are demanding more, and quite rightly so. We live in a dreadful estate that is bigger than any small town and yet the facilities are nil.'

On the other hand, Frances confirmed that the initial advantages of a new estate like Easterhouse included fresh air, a better outlook inside the home, better facilities than sharing an outside toilet with three families and having no hot water; the estate provided all of that about 35 years ago. The difficulty was that, in the eyes of the tenants, it was not followed up. Economies were made in every sector. There were no shops. Thirty-five years ago people did not demand so many things as they demand nowadays.

'Now,' she pointed out, 'they can watch on television, or read or see other people that have a nice pub, a nice restaurant, a nice supermarket, a picture hall, a swimming pool, and they can look at the whole of that area and say "why don't we get things like that?"'

To the question of whether it was possible to transform the whole place and create the kind of richer life that people are now aware of, Frances' answer was that, yes, it was possible—'through the people and through the partnership of the authorities and the government.'

So what happened to change things?

'Four years ago,' she said, 'we sat at the table for six months with the architects and they said, "what are the problems here?" and we made a list of basically 30 things that we felt were the problems as tenants. The committee did all the work, took it to all the tenants, came back and asked them to state in preference which one was the most important. The ones that came back the most important were the ones that were first improved in the property. They were insulation, wooden windows instead of metal and sound penetration which was the biggest problem. The sound penetration was serious. The houses are more anti-social than the tenants are.'

But the estate had many features that would not be found easily in an ordinary, modern housing scheme. The tenants had done wonderful things with the houses inside, and the estate had certain distinct social advantages. For example: 'The safety factor for children is that the tenants are looking out on where the children are playing, and anything that happens someone will quickly come down and do something about it.'

Peter McGurn, the architect for the scheme, was quite clear about the community aspects of the work. 'The architectural part of this particular case,' he said, 'was that we became involved from day one with the people, and we spent about a year talking to them and just developing the whole idea—the concept of the co-operative.'

The real need was to stabilise the community. It was a fundamental need. You couldn't stabilise the community so long as the housing stock and the environment were deteriorating, because people naturally wanted to get out. The essential need was to create a scenario by which people could develop an attitude of mind to the environment whereby they would want to stay.

Peter McGurn believed that what the people themselves were demonstrating was that 'if you pass the power, in a sense, into their hands and bag it out with money, then they can actually begin to resolve the problem in a decent environment.' He confirmed appalling sound levels as being one of the technical problems. You could hear people going to the toilet, or you could hear people having a domestic argument. Furthermore there was the problem of heat—the loss of heat through relatively thin wall construction. It was a problem to try to contain the heat and provide a thermal insulation equality within the houses. It was also important to change the proportion of housing types. There are different housing types now: 'Housing for single people, housing that is adapted for disabled people, housing geared now for older people, so there is a range of houses within the housing stock which, primarily before that, was just family housing, workers' housing.'

Nor were the problems confined to the houses themselves. Peter McGurn considered: 'You've got to control the territory outside the houses, and you've got to invest in that so that people ultimately

Below and right Children at Easterhouse, boys and girls, unimpressed and unworried by their environment, possibly thinking of the future when Easterhouse will be a 'perfect place to live in'.

maintain themselves and they know which territory belongs to them. If you talk to the Co-operative members you'll find there's a lifestyle within it and also a feeling among local folk now that they can control and influence their own affairs, and I think that is the fundamental thing. People should be in charge.'

When I remarked that he didn't, incidentally, look like an architect, he replied: 'Well, I hope I look like a human being.'

Jim Green, the housing manager for Easterhouse, had recently arrived from Lewisham. He is now the district housing manager with sole responsibility for the management of Easterhouse as an area. His first surprise, and a pleasant surprise, was to see that Easterhouse was fairly modern. The next surprise was to find that the whole housing estate was the same. 'If someone blind-folded you and dropped you off in a street you would have to walk to the corner to see where you are, because there are no distinguishing landmarks.' He was not altogether surprised by the condition of the buildings because he had been in housing for a long time. But he was surprised that for housing that was only 25 to 30 years old, the back court areas and the large green areas were in such very poor condition.

144

To my question: 'What do you think you can possibly achieve in an estate like this?' he replied:

> The best we can achieve is to make Easterhouse a perfect place to live and work in. You've got to be that way. Easterhouse can be pulled up by its bootlaces. It is not an inner city estate, it is a green field estate. At least two thirds of the area is surrounded by green fields. The town planning is poor to diabolical. If *that* can be put right we have the resources to put it right.

To the question: 'What is a perfect estate?' he replied:

> I think everybody has got their own interpretation, but to my mind, what I look for is that I have got a desirable home and a peaceful environment. To me, that's perfect. One of the advantages of Easterhouse is that they already have got a community. We need to make that community believe in where they live and most of them do already.

But what will they do? Jim Green says:

> I believe that in every large city there has been a lack of capital investment. Easterhouse is littered with the graveyards of previous improvements which have been under-funded and just gone. Put £10 000 in a back court in a back area there, come back in three months and it will be

eaten away. Back courts are now costing me a million pounds, but I tell you, I will come back in 30 years and it will still be there, and that's what you've got to do.

Looking on a wider prospectus, the council that is Glasgow has 164 000 houses, but I am impressed with what has happened at Calvay. It shows that tenants can manage themselves very, very effectively, and attract funding which is what we need today to make Easterhouse better.

In particular he says that the need was not for one system or one system of tenancy: you needed a good balance.

There is a place in Easterhouse for council tenants, and many folk enjoy being council tenants. There is a place for owner occupation, a hell of a lot more than we have today. There is a place for Co-operatives and I am also very interested in management co-operatives. There is a place for homesteading, for people who wish to build their own houses. One of the problems with today's Easterhouse, is that there is all one thing.

'Are there,' I asked, 'enough people to do the work?'

'Yes,' he replied, 'there are. We have to find them, they don't always jump up and raise their hands, but they are there.'

The lessons of Easterhouse and its record of remarkable activity and energy is that there cannot be any one answer to a housing problem. There must be different forms of tenancy, different forms of management and, I believe, different levels of cost. If to that you add different systems of construction, that is, different forms of technology, you have the beginning of a pluralistic system of housing.

This study has essentially been a historical one, from the 1840s to 1990. It has followed the story from philanthrophy combined with self-interest, to the onset of legislation; from there to organisation, and on to the vast housing schemes which have ended in a great muddle.

There are few subjects about which people feel more emotional, and few subjects about which people are, on the whole, more ignorant, despite being themselves the users of the product. Housing is not, after all, most people's priority. Answers to social surveys do not put housing first; it usually comes after education and health. On the other hand, there is no subject more politically loaded. People in charge have frequently felt guilty about their failure to solve the problem. Other people have felt idealistic about it, especially in the late nineteenth century and in the early twentieth century—for example, Addison, the Minister of Health, who resigned when finances were reduced in 1923. Now such enthusiasm comes not so much from government, but from voluntary organisations like Housing Associations and Co-operatives.

What this study has shown is that there are at least three, and possibly four, main areas of discussion about the future of housing. The first concerns architectural *design*—that is not just pretty façades, but the planning of houses that will satisfy people's needs functionally and make a pleasant, and possibly a pretty, place to live and express themselves.

What after all is a well designed *house*? It is a place which is convenient to live in, attractive to look at, easy to maintain, reasonable in cost and cheap to run. On the bigger social scale one might ask what represents good or well designed *housing*? It must include well designed houses, a convenient layout properly serviced, good management at an economical cost—the whole estate preferably humane in scale.

What changes all the time both for houses and housing is people's experience and their aspirations. There will never probably be a perfect house or perfect housing because the aspirations continually overtake the experience. There ought to be a formula—an equation—that relates the polarities of aspiration and satisfaction.

A second major item is the form of *tenure*—that is to say, the involvement of a person with his or her own house, whether they own it or borrow it, lease it or share it. Questions of tenancy are uppermost and are changing dramatically, and have done so in the last 100 years. The trend in Great Britain is towards 100 per cent owner-occupied housing. That will probably never be achieved and may not be desirable in any case. At present it looks as if something like 70 per cent of houses will eventually be owner-occupied, 20 per cent will be rented in various forms including council housing and 10 per cent may be rented privately. Recorded preferences in terms of user satisfaction show that there are considerable variations of attitude to the different types, depending on age groups.

What is clear overall is the need for rentable, affordable housing. The two adjectives go together because younger people starting a career may not be able, or even wish, to buy a house. And there is no apparent answer to the question of affordable and rentable housing for young, low paid people without subsidy. What therefore seems to be necessary is a partnership between public and private. The private area has, after all, the money, the public area has the power and responsibility. To bring the two together could only be beneficial for social housing. It may also be useful for Housing Associations, which form the third arm and look like being the major growth area in the organisation of tenancies in the future.

Thirdly, there are questions of *management*; that is, not just organisation but how well a property is looked after, maintained, protected and repaired day by day. This appears to be the most disastrous element in the public sector—notorious for carelessness and bureaucracy, the impersonal kind of management which effectively says 'take it or leave it'. In particular, maintenance has been a disaster. Costs in use have not been calculated and budgeted for in any local authority system. Lack of maintenance creates serious problems for the under-privileged and for the elderly. Nor is there any answer through the use of direct labour organisations, which notoriously cost a lot more than using local contractors.

Underlying all these factors is the fourth main area of discussion—the question of *money*. Have we enough money, or has there ever been enough money, to make decent housing for all people and to maintain it? That is a crucial question for the public sector. But it is not fundamentally different from the question for the private sector in a capitalist economy; everyone, both public and private, builds with borrowed money. A brief comment on the financing of the private sector may help to throw some light on the situation.

There are four main items in the cost of housing in the private sector. They are the cost of the house, the cost of the land it sits on, the builder's profits, and the cost of borrowing the money—the loan charges. What may be surprising to many people is that the cost of the house is far from being in most cases the major cost. To take an example from the Yorkshire village in which I live and in which new stone-fronted houses are at present being built for sale, the selling prices are in the region of £100 000 to £120 000. I have compared my own experience as an architect with that of several local builders and we agree that it is impossible that the actual cost of building such a house can be more than £40 000. The remaining £80 000 or so is made up from three other factors.

Builders' profits are notoriously difficult to discover. But figures published in 1988 in *Building* suggest that among some of the major contractors the profit on a house will vary from £4000 to £12 000. Given the huge housing programmes of such contractors, this adds up to a very considerable sum. Major contractors confirm that housing is more profitable than contracting.

The other two factors are crucial. The repayment of a loan in the form of a mortgage will normally add up to a sum of three or more times the original loan. What is much more variable—and ultimately definitive—is the cost of the land. It is, and probably always has been, the major factor in price differences between otherwise similar houses. The land on which the house sits may represent less than 15 per cent of the total cost in parts of Scotland. It represents more— sometimes vastly more—than 50 per cent of the cost in London.

When all these factors are taken into consideration it is obvious that minor savings made by a designer—sometimes after hours of struggling with areas and materials—may be almost irrelevant to the final cost. In the public sector, where the cost of the loans and the land are massive sums, attempts to reduce the cost of a house can easily be swamped by the other factors. It has for a long time seemed to me absurd and possibly iniquitous that dwellings may be reduced to a cost which makes them substandard (and eventually uninhabitable) when the real costs that ought to be reduced are elsewhere. It may be that we have been controlling (and subsidising) the wrong elements. Nothing can take away from the need for a good habitable dwelling for all. As Disraeli remarked in the nineteenth century: 'We all eat enough and some of us drink a great deal too much, but this I will venture to say that no man can be too well-housed.'

As this book is being completed and the television programmes on which it is based are being made, the future of housing is being affected by legislation whose long-term effects it is impossible to predict. That legislation is intended, according to its promoters: firstly, to reverse the decline and improve the quality of rented housing; secondly, to give council tenants the right to choose their own landlord; thirdly, to aim public money at the most acute problems; and fourthly, to encourage the growth of owner-occupation.

The policy of the present government includes not only the liberalisation of the housing market and the maximisation of consumer choice, but the removal of housing from the control of local authorities—that is from their traditional role as providers of housing. If the local authority loses control of housing, as it has already lost, or looks like losing, control of education and health, this will make a major difference to the social structure of the country. The local authority was founded, after all, to deal with order and refuse—drains and policemen—and it may end up doing something similar again. But does the local authority wish to divest itself of housing? The answer varies from authority to authority.

Housing has always been bedevilled by politics and it may be that the latest moves will make things worse. It appears that the essence of the changes are as follows: firstly, to subsidise people rather than property and to create, therefore, an ordinary market for all the people; and secondly, to oblige society to support those who cannot manage to support themselves in terms of housing. That obligation has always been difficult to judge. Overall it appears that local authorities will become enablers rather than providers.

The only comprehensive report to look at the whole of housing, including private and public, was the report chaired by the Duke of Edinburgh and published in 1985. The report made two fundamental recommendations: on the one hand, winding up of housing benefit for tenants and of mortgage tax relief for owner-occupiers. On the other, replacing the housing component in supplementary benefit with a needs-related housing allowance. The calculations of both costs and savings involved on both sides suggest that these changes could be made with considerable benefit but with no extra cost to the public. The distribution of financial help would be fairer to those in greatest need of help with their housing.

The recommendations are so simple and so obviously sensible that there is little likelihood of them ever being put into practice. The needs-related housing allowance is the central aspect of the committee's recommendations. It would be made available to all those on low or limited incomes to allow them to pay for the housing they require. Giving assistance in cash rather than offering a particular dwelling would help to provide a greater choice between owning and renting, between homes of different qualities and those provided by different landlords. The gradual withdrawal of mortgage tax relief is a crucial feature of the changes. The Prime Minister has so far said that she has no intention of letting it happen.

The purpose of the report was to create fairness between local authority tenants, Housing Associations and private landlords—to create tenant choice, to encourage letting of unoccupied property and to attract large-scale investment by assessing rents at a rate that ensured a reasonable return. By stimulating private investment the committee hoped to reduce the dependence of social housing agencies on government subsidy, and by providing a decent return for landlords, encourage them to modernise low grade property.

The report stressed the need for increased flexibility, variety and sensitivity in housing management. It supported wider tenant participation and consultation, with the occasional transfer of property to alternative landlords such as Housing Co-operatives. It deplored the lack of priority given to housing, as well as the tendency to blame bad conditions on those who suffered from them. It stated: 'While our proposals do not require a big increase in public expenditure they do demand changes in legislation, and financial arrangements to allow private sector resources to be attracted on a much wider scale than heretofore.' Its objective, it said, was 'to change permanently the basis upon which society meets housing needs'.

So what is needed for a better housing future? Three main courses suggest themselves: firstly, a drastic governmental change such as that suggested by the Duke of Edinburgh's inquiry; secondly, a drastic improvement and, where necessary, demolition of hopelessly substandard housing; and thirdly, encouragement of good housing, mostly through Housing Associations. The knowledge and the skills are available. What is missing is sufficient energy, encouragement and, of course, money.

The housing question cannot be answered for two basic reasons. It is not one question, but a whole series of questions, to which there must, therefore, be a whole series of answers; and it is not one huge problem, but a vast set of smaller problems requiring a corresponding set of answers. And there can never be a final solution in our society, because people's expectations always exceed the provision available. At the beginning of the century the possession of a bathroom was an aspiration. Nowadays that is taken for granted; many people aspire to bathrooms *en suite*. At the beginning of the century the family house was the major demand, now the demand is for smaller, more varied dwellings.

What improvements can most easily be made for the future? The most obvious improvement is that people should be involved with the management as well as the design of their dwellings. This already happens in the commissioning of private houses; local authority tenants need, and are starting to exercise, that right. Steps must be taken to eliminate overcrowding and uncomfortable conditions. And there is a need to set higher standards for the clearance and replacement of housing stock.

But what are the positive signs of improvement and change? In future subsidies will be paid to people rather than to buildings, and that will enable people to have more choice. It should also enable people to take more responsibility for their own housing. There is no longer a case for mass housing, but there is an unmistakable case for organisations which will be responsible for smaller schemes of housing—a pluralistic system of housing management.

In the end, fundamental to all housing must be the work and the attitude of the local authorities. Until recently they have been providing the major part of new housing and have been responsible for at least six million houses. Their position has changed. In the fifties and sixties they were building bigger and higher. In the seventies they repented and changed their policies. In the eighties they have been pursuing alternative policies for lower, more dispersed and different kinds of housing. In the nineties they may demolish the high buildings and cut down the remainders to suit special needs.

There is a good deal of evidence leading to a conclusion which several experienced planners and managers of housing do not reject. That is the general proposition that it would be both socially and economically best if all council houses were *given* to their tenants. The new owners would become responsible for the maintenance and repair of their houses. The local authorities would avoid the huge bills expected for maintenance and would at the same time save on administrative costs, the bureaucracy of the housing departments.

For the majority of ordinary two and three-storey houses such a change would present no real problem. The problems are with the mass schemes, the walk-up blocks and the tower blocks. But forms of co-operative ownership are already being developed for those blocks: and Housing Associations—if necessary devoted to a single block and composed of the present tenants—could take over the management and costs. They probably will in any case as a result of the new Housing Act. It is not difficult to visualise a scene of housing almost all of which is owner-occupied, either individually or by a community.

What seem clear are three general conclusions. First of all, that the rehabilitation of existing houses, their improvement, is best for the poor and for the starters, and also good for cities and towns. It uses existing stock, it tries to preserve existing communities, it tries to protect extended families and to enable people to be part of a continuity rather than part of a clean sweep and a new estate. Secondly, there is no doubt that community architecture is beginning to make sense. That is an architecture which has the tenant or occupier as the client. It can be a programme of self-building, or joint management by the tenants, the designers and the owners. It is happening already in London, in the docklands and elsewhere, and the evidence is that it can be very positive and very satisfying. Thirdly, there is no doubt of the advantage when the tenants take responsibility. Co-operatives such as that at Easterhouse are good examples of it. Housing Associations and self-build systems are equally beneficial. Active participants in the management of their housing may be rare, but there is a good deal of evidence that more people can be found. That does not remove the need for managers and designers; what is clear is that the occupiers can play a greater part in the protection and organisation of their own environment.

If it were not for the cost of the land and the cost of servicing loans, it would certainly be technically possible for satisfactory houses to be designed for families on lower than average incomes. What makes it impossible is the high cost of land, particularly in cities, and the cost of servicing the loans. It seems one of the ironies of history that any programme that considers the nationalisation of the means of manufacture, distribution and trade, has nevertheless never resolved the one basic element to which all people have a right, which is the land on which they live. There is little doubt, in terms of the total cost of housing, that if the cost of the land could be resolved, it would be possible to provide good houses for everyone.

Meantime in any place like Easterhouse on the edge of Glasgow, it is worth looking at what is already happening. The work at Easterhouse is a community effort, community enterprise. And it must be community enterprise that lies at the heart of any solution to the current housing question.

What must surely happen is a new partnership between the more articulate members of the community and the professionals whose responsibility it is to solve the problem—creative collaboration between public and private for the benefit of everyone.

As we look at the way in which we've housed people, both throughout history and in our own time, we have to accept that we have never spent enough on it. In the end, all such projects depend upon money and upon control. Whatever the local enthusiasm, it must ultimately be the responsibility of those in power to provide the conditions and the support that will enable local initiatives to provide a solution. In the final analysis we must accept that housing means homes for people, preferably with the people in charge.

BIBLIOGRAPHY

ABERCROMBIE, P. *Town and country planning* 3rd ed. Oxford University Press, 1959. op.

ABRAMS, C. *Housing in the modern world* Faber, 1966; 1969. op.

ALLAUN, F. *No place like home: Britain's housing tragedy (from the victim's view) and how to overcome it* Deutsch, 1972. op.

ASHWORTH, H.I. *Flats: design and equipment* Pitman, 1936. op.

AUDIT COMMISSION FOR LOCAL AUTHORITIES IN ENGLAND AND WALES. *Performance review in local government* 8 vols. HMSO, 1986.

BARRETT, H. & PHILLIPS, J. *Suburban style: the British home 1840–1960* Macdonald, 1987.

BAZLINGTON, C. ed. *Inquiry into British housing* National Federation of Housing Associations, 1985.

BEERBOHM, M. *And even now* Heinemann, 1920. op.

BELL, C. & BELL, R. *City Fathers: the early history of town planning in Britain* Barrie & Rockliff, 1969. op.

BERRY, F. *Housing: the great British Failure* Knight, 1974. op.

BOWLEY, M. *Housing and the state 1919–1944* Allen & Unwin, 1945. op.; Garland, New York, 1985.

BRETT, C.E.B. *Housing a divided community* Queens University Belfast, 1987. op.

BURNETT, J. *A social history of housing 1815–1985* 2nd r.e. Methuen, 1986.

CHAPMAN, S.D. ed. *The history of working class housing: a symposium* David & Charles, 1971. op.

CHERRY, G.E. *The politics of town planning* Longman, 1982. op.

CHERRY, G.E. *Town planning in its social context* L. Hill, 1970. op.

CIVIC TRUST. *Civic Trust Awards report* Civic Trust, published annually.

COLEMAN, A.M. *Utopia on trial: vision and reality in planned housing* H. Shipman, 1985.

COONEY, E.W. *Ways and means of housing provision 1850–1986* Business Archives Council, proceedings of annual conference, 1986.

COONEY, E.W. *Problems of housing and social progress* York University, 1988.

COX, G.M. *The circle of despair* Shelter, 1973. op.

CORBUSIER, L. *My work* trans. by James Palmes. Architectural Press, 1961. op.

CORBUSIER, L. *Towards a new architecture* trans. by Frederick Etchells. Architectural Press, 1970.

CREESE, W.L. ed. *The legacy of Raymond Unwin: a human*

pattern for planning M.I.T., 1967.
CREESE, W.L. *The search for environment: the garden city: before and after* Yale University Press, 1966. op.

DAUNTON, M.J. *House and home in the Victorian city: working class housing 1850–1914* (Studies in Urban History) E. Arnold, 1983.

DONNISON, D.V. *The government of housing* Penguin, 1967. op.

DUNLEAVY, P. *The politics of mass housing in Britain 1945–1975: study of corporate power and professional influence in the welfare state* Oxford University Press, 1981.

ESHER, L.B. *A broken wave: the rebuilding of England 1940–1980* Allen Lane, 1981; Penguin, 1983. op.

FORSHAW, J.H. & ABERCROMBIE, P. *County of London plan* Macmillan, 1943. op.

GELFAND, M.D., et al. eds. *Half a century of municipal decline 1935–1985* Allen & Unwin, 1985.

GREENWOOD, W. *Love on the dole* Penguin, 1969.

GREVE, J. *London's homeless* Codicate Press, 1964. op.

HAMNETT, C. & RANDOLPH, B. *Cities, housing and profits* Hutchinson, 1988.

HEALTH, MINISTRY OF. *Design of Dwellings. Report of the Design of Dwellings Sub-committee of the Ministry of Health Central Advisory Committee* HMSO, 1944. op. *Homes for today and tomorrow. Report of a sub-committee of the Central Housing Advisory Committee* HMSO, 1961.

HOWARD, E. *Garden cities of tomorrow* r.e. Attic Books, 1985.

HUNTER, D.R. *The slums: challenge and response* Free Press of Glencoe, Collier-Macmillan, 1964, 1968. op.

JONES, afterwards CHESTERTON, A.E. *I lived in a slum* Gollancz, 1936; Queensway Press, 1937. op.

KNEVITT, C. & WATES, N. *Community architecture* Penguin, 1987.

MAC FADYEN, D. *Sir Ebenezer Howard and the Garden City Movement* Manchester University Press, 1933. op.

MALPASS, P. ed. *The housing crisis* Croom Helm, 1986.

MALPASS, P. & MURIE, A. *Housing policy and practice* 2nd ed. Macmillan, 1987.

MERRETT, S. *State housing in Britain* Routledge & Kegan Paul, 1979. op.

MOWAT, C.L. *Britain between the wars 1918–1940* Methuen, 1968.

MUMFORD, L. *The culture of cities* Secker & Warburg, 1938. op.

MURIE, A. & JEFFERS, S. eds. *Living in bed and breakfast: the experience of homelessness in London* (School of Advanced Urban Studies working paper no. 71.) Bristol University, 1987.

NORTHERN IRELAND HOUSING EXECUTIVE. *House, home and design* Architectural Publications, 1988.

NUTTGENS, P. *The landscape of ideas* Faber, 1972. op.

OSBORN, F.J. *Green-belt cities* Evelyn, Adams & Mackay, 1969. op.

PAHL, R.E. *Divisions of Labour* Blackwell, 1984.

PAHL, R.E. ed. *Readings in urban sociology* Pergamon Press, 1968. op.

PANTON, J.E. *From kitchen to garret – hints for young householders* Ward & Downey, 1890; 1893. op.

PARIS, C. & BLACKABY, B. *Not much improvement: urban renewal policy in Birmingham* Heinemann, 1979. op.

PAWLEY, M. *Architecture versus housing* (New concepts of architecture) Studio Vista, 1971. op.

PIKE, E.R. *Human documents of the Victorian golden age* Allen & Unwin, 1974. op.

RICHARDS, J.M. *Castles on the ground: the anatomy of suburbia* 2nd ed. J. Murray, 1973. op.

ROBERTS, R. *The classic slum: Salford life in the first quarter of the century* n.e. Penguin, 1973.

ROBINSON, W. HEATH & BROWNE, K.R.G. *How to live in a flat* Hutchinson, 1936; Duckworth, 1976. op.

ROWNTREE, B.S. *Poverty: a study of town life* (The English working class no. 21). Garland, 1980. op.

ROWNTREE, B.S. *Poverty and progress: a second social survey of York* Longman, 1941. op.

RUSKIN, J. *Sesame and Lilies* People's Library, 1907; Dent, 1953. op.

SAUNDERS, P. *The significance of the home in contemporary English social life* (Paper presented at the conference on *The sociology of consumption*, University of Oslo, 1988).

SHARP, T. *Town planning* Penguin, 1940. op.

SHELTER HOUSING ADVICE CENTRE *Housing progress report* SHAC. Published annually.

SHELTER HOUSING ADVICE CENTRE *Housing facts and figures* 3rd ed. SHAC, 1980. op.

SIMON, E. *How to abolish the slums* Longman, 1929. op.

SMITH, M.E.H. *A guide to housing* Housing Centre Trust, 1977.

STRETTON, H. *Capitalism, socialism and the environment* Cambridge University Press, 1976.

SWENARTON, M. *Homes fit for heroes: the politics and architecture of early state housing in Britain* Heinemann, 1981.

TARN, J.N. *Five per cent philanthropy: an account of housing in urban areas between 1840 and 1914* Cambridge University Press, 1973. op.

THOMPSON, P. *The work of William Morris* Heinemann, 1967. op.

TUBBS, R. *Living in cities* Penguin, 1942. op.

TUDOR WALTERS REPORT *Report of local government boards from England, Wales and Scotland no. 391.* 1918.

UNWIN, R. *Nothing gained by overcrowding* Garden Cities & Town Planning Association, 3rd ed., 1918. op.

UNWIN, R. *Town planning in practice: an introduction to the art of designing cities and suburbs* Fisher Unwin, 1909. op. *Village homes for village people* NAC, 1987. op.

WARD, M. and WARD, N. *Home in the 20's and 30's* I. Allen, 1978. op.

WILLMOTT, P. *Social polarisation and social housing* Policy Studies Institute, 1988.

WORSDALL, F. *The tenement – a way of life: a social historical and architectural study of housing in Glasgow* Chambers, 1979. op.

YORKE, F.R.S. *The modern flat* 3rd ed. Architectural Press, 1950. op.

INDEX

PICTURE CREDITS
Leeds City Council pages 62, 64, 65 and 92; Northern Ireland Housing Executive page 117; Syndication International page 83; Wilkinson, Hindle, Halsall, Lloyd Partnership pages 106 and 107. The remaining photographs were taken for the BBC by John Warwick, with assistance from Paul Otter and Kevin Robertson.